The Philosophi Antholog_

Volume 1

Philosophy of Religion

Looking into the nature and existence of God as well as wider religious concepts and ideas.

Thank you for your purchase of the Philosophy Vibe Anthology. Your support of the channel is very much appreciated, and I hope Philosophy Vibe has helped you on your philosophical journey.

-    Charles Georgiou

Contents

Introduction

George: Hello and welcome to the Philosophy Vibe anthology, a collection of scripts from the Philosophy Vibe YouTube channel. This book will focus on the philosophy of religion.

John: Excellent.

George: Philosophy of religion is an examination of the ideas and concepts surrounding God and wider religious beliefs. Through the course of this book we will look into various arguments for the existence God, an in-depth analysis into the concept and nature of God, as well as deep discussions into broader religious ideas. We hope you enjoy.

John: Great, let's begin.

George: Very well.

Chapter I

The Nature & Existence of God

The Nature of God

George: We shall begin by looking into the concept and the nature of God. Now, philosophy of religion is centred around God, so it's good just to pull back and understand, what do we mean when we are talking about God? So then John, if someone was to ask you to describe God, what would you say?

John: Well, I would refer to Him as the creator. A supreme being that created the entire universe.

George: Yes, good, that is the common understanding within the Judeo-Christian belief in God. He's seen as the creator of everything, the creator of the heavens and the universe, of life as we know it. Now, do you think this is a reasonable belief to have?

John: Well, yes.

George: Why?

John: So, we can see, life exists, the universe exists and this had to come from somewhere. It seems reasonable to argue then there must be a being who existed before the universe, and was able to bring the universe into existence. And that being we know of as God.

George: Exactly. Everything we see here today must have come from somewhere. And many religions hold that this came from God. As there was nothing before God, if He created everything this would mean God created everything ex nihilo, so God created the whole universe out of nothing.

John: Right.

George: However isn't there a problem here?

John: What?

George: If God created everything out of nothing, then who in fact created God?

John: Well here is where I would have to agree with Aristotle. God is the Unmoved Mover.

George: What's that?

John: The universe is contingent, it is forever changing and is dependent on something else for its existence; it could quite possibly not have existed if circumstances were different. So in order for this to come into existence it needs a being to cause the motion and start the whole thing off. However this being itself cannot have been caused by anything otherwise there would just be an infinite regress. So God is a being who can move other things but He was not moved by anything prior, as there was not anything prior. God Himself is uncaused yet He is the being which caused everything else. The original craftsman He built everything and nothing built Him.

George: Ok I understand. And from there is it right to agree that as He created everything, created the motion and all the laws of nature that govern the universe, He is actually all powerful He is omnipotent He is not bound by any natural laws as He is the one who creates these laws.

John: Yes exactly.

George: And as He is all powerful this would mean that He is able to be omniscient, to know everything that is.

John: Yes.

George: And it would allow Him to be omnipresent, God can be absolutely everywhere all the time.

John: Correct. This is the common Judeo-Christian understanding of God, the creator of everything, an unmoved mover who is an all-powerful being.

George: Is it then fair to argue that, as God is the creator of everything He is therefore responsible for everything that happens.

John: Well you could say that all the laws of nature and how our planet functions, He is responsible for. As He set these laws in motion. However when it comes to human choices many argue that God gave humans free will the ability to choose their own actions. This would then make us responsible for our own actions, not God. And we could not expect God to intervene as this would contradict free will.

George: Very interesting point. Let's then look at God and morality for a second. The bible claims that God is benevolent, so He is all loving. He wants people to act in the best way and he wants people to be happy. And because God knows everything He then knows what it means to be morally perfect.

John: Yes, so because of this God becomes the source of human ethics. He can tell us what is right and what is wrong. Because he is all powerful and all knowing He knows the perfect way to behave. And because of this He becomes the law giver. He gives humans the code to live by, He tells us how we should act. We then derive our morals from God who is the supremely perfect being.

George: Ok that makes sense, however does the Euthyphro dilemma not create complications for this belief.

John: What's that?

George: The Euthyphro dilemma simply asks, 'is what is morally good commanded by God because it is morally good. Or is it morally good because it is commanded by God".

John: Hmmm.

George: Either morality exists above and beyond God or, or morality is just created by God and is just an arbitrary expression of his desire.

John: Interesting.

George: We shall look into this a little later on but for now let's look into one of the major problems for the existence of God.

* RANDOM CHOICE/WHIM RATHER THAN REASON (CAPRICIOUS/WHIMSICAL)

The Problem of Evil

George: One of the biggest problems a theist must face when arguing for the existence of God is the problem of evil. Now, there are two types of evil that exist, we have moral evil, that is evil that human beings do to each other, things like murder. And natural evil, bad that nature creates like hurricanes and tsunamis. The existence of both of these make a lot of problems for Judeo-Christian belief in God. John, would you like to raise the argument.

John: Ok, so essentially we know God to be an all-loving all-powerful and all-knowing being, if this is the case why is there evil? If God loved us He would not want humans to suffer, if He knew everything He would know all the evil that exists, and if He is all powerful He can stop it. So why is there evil?

George: Ok I see the problem and I'm going to try and solve it with the Augustinian Theodicy. St Augustine argues that God did create the perfect world, the exact world that a benevolent and omnipotent God would be expected to make. God never created evil, rather evil is just a privation of goodness, like darkness is the privation of light, it is not something that is created it is just the absence of something else.

LOSS/ABSENCE

John: Right.

George: Augustine then refers to the Bible and the book of Genesis, a perfect world where humans were given free will, as we saw within the story of Adam and Eve. God loves the humans and wants humans to accept Him, so by giving them freewill it will allow humans the will and the choice to either accept God or reject Him. Unfortunately Adam and Eve ate from the forbidden tree of knowledge and rejected God. They turned their back on Him and His goodness and their punishment brought about the evil we know of today. Once Adam and Eve committed the original sin the world became distant from God and His goodness, therefore evil flourished. Moral evil occurred because of man's disobedience and bad choices, natural evil occurs because of nature turning against us and punishing us for our rejection of God. And as we were all present in the loins of Adam, we must all suffer and live with evil as punishment.

John: Wow that seems pretty extreme, seems like God is not someone you want to upset.

George: Well Augustine says He does give man a second chance, and that is by following the path of Jesus Christ and accepting Jesus you can be let back into paradise. So God still does love us and wants us all to go back to Him and choose Him again.

John: Well that's good to know.

George: So then if we accept the Augustinian Theodicy we can see God does love us, He did create a perfect world where He wanted us to love Him back and accept Him, however it was human free will that lead to the original sin. Which therefore means it was humans who brought about the evil in our world, not God, and every human must now deal with it, allowing the existence of an omnibenevolent God along with evil in the world

John: Wait a minute not so fast. There seems to be a lot of problems with the Augustinian theodicy.

George: Like what?

John: Well firstly it seems contradictory to say that God created the perfect world, yet it was still possible for evil to exist. How can this be, surely if the world was perfect it would be impossible for evil to ever exist no matter what happened? This argument was raised by Schleiermacher; how can a perfect world have the possibility of evil, it is a logical contradiction. Either the world was never perfect to begin with, or if it was perfect then it means God purposely created evil, which Augustine said He didn't. So which is it? Either way it does not sound like something an all loving God would do.

George: Good point.

John: Also it was only Adam and Eve who disobeyed God, yet all humans have had to suffer with evil. This does not sound like something an all loving God would do, why should I be punished for something that the very first human had done.

George: Yes I see.

John: And finally, the whole Theodicy relies on genesis and the story of Adam and Eve as a fact. This story is inconsistent with scientific discoveries into the origins of humans and with the evolution of people and of nature. So this throws the whole Theodicy into doubt, and so does not help solve the problem of evil argument.

George: Ok let me try another argument on you then.

John: Go for it.

George: The Irenaean theodicy, or as Hick later referred to it, the soul-making theodicy. The argument claims that God did in fact create the possibility of evil however He done it for a soul making purpose. In order for good to exist, evil has to exist, if humans only lived in a world of good, we would never be able to recognise it. We can only recognise tall if we know what it means to be short, we can only recognise cold if we know what it's like to be hot, and so we can only recognise good if we know what evil is. Evil is therefore necessary in appreciating good.

John: Yes I understand that.

George: The soul-making theodicy then claims that God did not make humans perfect, rather He purposely made them imperfect but gave them free will in order for humans to reach perfection through their own free choices. And in order for them to achieve perfection they must make the right choices to get there, this makes it so much more worthwhile and special than just being created perfect. However, in order for there to be the good choices it means there must exist bad choices and these bad choices, which some people choose, is what causes evil. So the existence of evil is necessary in the path to achieving moral perfection, it helps us grow, it makes our soul. This then shows that evil can exist and God can still be all loving and all powerful.

John: Again there are a lot of problems with this argument too.

George: Like what?

John: Well firstly it really only accounts for moral evil. So yes I can see that with free will man must have the choice of evil. But why does the natural world have to be so evil? Why does there have to be earthquakes, tsunamis, diseases? This causes so much suffering, why did God have to create such a harsh planet to live on. This doesn't seem like something an all loving all powerful God would do.

George: Yes I see the problem.

John: And, if we're just focusing on moral evil, why is it so unbalanced.

George: What do you mean?

John: There are people who go through life having had some really bad stuff happen to them, and other people who have never really suffered. If evil is necessary in making everyone's soul why does everyone not experience it in the same amounts.

George: Ok I got it.

John: I don't think the soul making theodicy is sufficient in solving the problem of evil.

George: Right ok, there's one last thing I want to touch on before we finish. What was central to both the

Augustinian theodicy and the Irenean soul-making theodicy?

John:　　　　Free will.

George:　　　Yes exactly, free will. Both theodicies shift the blame of evil onto people rather than God. We see how evil is the result of human choices and God is still benevolent and wants people to do good, and He is still omnipotent, but He just cannot intervene, as soon as God intervenes it no longer becomes free will as God is therefore controlling what humans do. Do you think free will defence is sufficient in itself to address the problem of evil?

John:　　　　No I don't.

George:　　　Why?

John:　　　　Well firstly as we saw with the Irenean theodicy it can only explain moral evil, it does nothing for natural evil.

George:　　　Yes we saw that.

John:　　　　Also, I personally don't see a logical contradiction in having humans who freely choose but only choose good. A similar point was raised by JL Mackie. Think about it, we have humans now who are faced with choices and freely choose good, so there is no contradiction in God creating all humans like this all the time, we all would have freedom to choose wrong but we never make that choice, if He was all powerful He could do this, and if He was all loving He would do this.

George: Ok.

John: And lastly I think that God's omniscience poses a threat to free will in general.

George: Explain.

John: Well, if God knows everything then He knows the future, and if you know the future then you know how an event is going to turn out before it has happened. So if you know how an event is going to turn out then it sort of means that it is pre-determined. Let's go back to the Augustinian Theodicy and look at Adam and Eve.

George: Ok.

John: If God is all knowing and can see into the future, He would have known that Adam and Eve were going to eat from the forbidden tree before He had even created them. So their sin was established before they were even created, how then were they ever free not to choose what they chose. It then seems God purposely created Adam and Eve with an intended destiny to commit the original sin which would not make Him benevolent. Or Adam and Eve did freely choose the sin but God just had no idea it was going to happen then he is not omniscient nor omnipotent.

George: Very interesting argument. So there you go the problem of evil with the existence of God. Let us now look into the three traditional arguments for the existence of God.

The Ontological Argument

George: The first argument is known as the ontological argument. The ontological argument is a popular argument amongst theists as it intends to prove the existence of God through a priori logic. It basically says, God exists and this can be proven by the very concept of God Himself.

John: Interesting.

George: The ontological argument was first put forward by St Anselm of Canterbury. Anselm argued that we all share a common understanding and concept of God, he described this as 'That than which nothing greater can be thought of'. So the greatest possible being that could exist, there is nothing greater that can be conceived.

John: Yes, fair enough I agree, that is the common understanding of God.

George: Well now if you agree with that then Anselm argues you are a fool if you do not believe God exists.

John: Why is that?

George: Let me ask you, what is greater, the concept of a pencil in someone's mind that doesn't actually exist, on an actual real pencil that does exist.

John: Well obviously the real pencil is greater than a concept of a pencil in someone's mind, as that pencil only exists in the mind whereas the real pencil exists in reality,

George: Exactly, so then think about it, we agreed the concept of God is that than which nothing greater can be thought of, so then if it is greater to exist in reality than in the mind, then God has to exist in reality, otherwise He is not the greatest possible being. How could the greatest possible being only exist in the mind? That means things that actually exist are greater, but that is a logical contradiction as you cannot think of something greater than the greatest being. So by the very definition and concept of God, His existence cannot be reasonably denied. So using this logic you can see God does exist.

John: Wait, wait, I can't agree with that.

George: Why?

John: You could use that very same logic to prove anything exists, even things we know don't exist.

George: Show me.

John: Ok I'm going to use the example by the Benedictine monk Gaunilo, he said using the ontological argument he could prove the existence of the perfect lost island filled with jewels and riches. Think about it, I have an idea of the greatest island, it's always greater to exist in reality, therefore the perfect greatest island possible exists in reality, it's nonsense as we know there is no such thing.

George: Well now hold on I don't think Gaunilo's argument is that damaging to the ontological argument.

John: Really?

George: Well yes think about it, an island is a contingent thing, it is not at all contradictory to imagine the non-existence of any island whether perfect or not, and so if the non-existence of the island is possible then it cannot be the greatest possible thing, an island can only be relatively perfect in comparison to another island, it's not the greatest thing ever. Whereas Anselm is saying the concept of God is that which nothing greater can be conceived. And so if the non-existence of God was possible, then He wouldn't be that greatest possible being, because of this Anselm argues God must necessarily exist, He has to exist in every possible world or possible universe, God's existence must be present it logically has to.

John: Ok I see.

George: Following on from that point Descartes expanded the ontological argument and argued in a very similar way to Anselm. He basically said, thinking of God as not existing is just as contradictory as thinking of a triangle without three sides. We have a concept of a triangle, and part of the concept of a triangle is that it has three sides, for you to say you are thinking of a triangle but it doesn't have three sides it means you are not thinking of a triangle, if you're thinking of a triangle it has to have three sides. Descartes then describes God as a supremely perfect being, and to be perfect means you must have necessary existence, if you do not have necessary existence then you are not supremely perfect. So if the concept of God is a supremely perfect being then by the very concept it means He necessarily exists.

John: No I think Descartes and Anselm still have a fundamental flaw in their logic.

George: Ok, explain.

John: Well it was Kant who raised this argument. He said, using Descartes example, it is contradictory to think of a triangle without three sides, but it is not contradictory to deny the existence of a triangle and its three sides, and just say that nothing like that exists. So then you may say, if God is supremely perfect he exists, but I could say God does not exist neither does his perfection, I'm denying the whole concept.

George: Yes I see.

John: Kant also goes on and says that Descartes is making another mistake by claiming that existence is a predicate, in fact existence is not a predicate and should never be used as such.

George: What do you mean?

John: You can have a concept of something, and attach predicates to it, let's say Santa Claus, I have a concept of him, and the predicates he has are, he's fat, he has a white beard he dresses in red etc. Now existence adds nothing new to concept of Santa, it tells us nothing about the concept of Santa as it is not a predicate, whether he exists or not the concept is the same.

George: Right.

John: So then if existence is not a predicate, it therefore cannot be part of the concept of something and so it cannot be an analytical preposition. Existence then is synthetic, it relies on evidence to be affirmed, so it is a posteriori. Therefore the ontological argument tries to make existence part of the concept of God, and so commits a big mistake as existence is not a predicate it cannot be part of the concept of God but rather it is something that needs to be externally verified, we need to go beyond the concept to prove God's existence, it is not part of the concept.

George: Yes I see the problem.

John: And finally, I would like to raise Aquinas' objection. He argued that as humans we cannot ever know, or be certain of the correct concept of God, as mere mortals we cannot truly know, and so how can we attempt to prove anything using the concept of God. Taking both Aquinas' and Kant's criticisms into account I have to say that I do not think the ontological argument proves the existence of God.

George: Very well argued. We will be returning to the ontological argument a little later but for now let's move on to the second traditional argument for the existence of God.

The Teleological Argument

George: Moving on to the Teleological Argument. Now, the teleological argument is an argument that tries to prove the existence of God through a focus on the design of our world. It is also referred to as the design argument. In short it claims that because of the complexity of our world and our universe, some thinking being needed to design it. Look how complex the human body is, look how precise and well balanced our planet is making it able for us to live and grow. If the world was even slightly different, we would not be able to exist on it. It is so well put and intricately put together, so much order and regularity that there needs to be a designer. And this designer is God.

John: Well you reached that conclusion pretty quickly.

George: Ok let me explain it in a bit more depth. Now the word teleological comes from the Greek word Telos, which means end, or purpose or goal, and that is the fundamental principle of the teleological argument, everything has a goal.

John: In what way?

George: If something has a purpose then it must have been designed in order to have this purpose, in order to move and act to this specific goal. This was advocated by St Thomas Aquinas. Aquinas had 5 ways of proving the existence of God, his fifth way is considered to be the teleological argument. Aquinas argues that every non intelligent thing in our world has its own purpose, a goal it tends to and it follows through natural law. If we look at a specific flower, if given sun light and water it will grow vertical, we can take a different flower and again with sun and water it grows vertical. It's this direction and purpose of the flower following strict laws of nature, it always has the same end always has the same Telos.

John:　　　Ok.

George:　　　Now would you agree that something that lacks knowledge, an unintelligent thing cannot fulfil a purpose unless it is guided by something with knowledge. Aquinas used the example of an archer and his bow and arrows. Imagine the unintelligent bow and arrow without the archer, it's just a bit of wood and string sitting there. In order for this to achieve its purpose and do what it was meant to do, it needs the archer to place the arrow onto the bow and shoot it. As though, in order for the bow and arrow to reach its purpose it needs an intelligent being, someone with knowledge to guide it right.

John:　　　Yes.

George:　　　Well then, most of nature is unintelligent, yet nature itself has a purpose, everything within nature is following a direction. So then if every unintelligent thing needs an intelligent being to guide it, then it seems that nature, our world and our universe needs an intelligent being to give it this direction, to give everything its purpose, and this being is what we call God.

John:　　　Right I see

George: The Teleological Argument was further developed by William Paley who argued from two points of view, design of purpose and design of regularity, and he did this with his watch analogy. Paley is taking a walk one day and he notices a rock on the floor. He quickly wonders to himself, where did that rock come from and then quickly concludes it just came from nature, it could have probably been lying there forever. Paley carries on walking and then notices a watch on the floor. He picks up the watch and sees how brilliantly it has been crafted, the dials and the cogs, all shaped and fashioned to give this object a specific purpose of telling the time. Paley then wonders how this watch got here, but he does not conclude the same of the watch as he done of the stone. The complexity of the watch and its clear purpose, means someone with knowledge designed this. Someone with knowledge took these materials and created this watch for a specific purpose, it is too complicated to have just appeared by chance or by nature, the watch has a designer, would you agree?

John: Well yes, if I found a watch I would obviously think this has been designed and created by someone.

George: Exactly, but then our world, our universe, is a trillion times more intricate and complex than a watch, so why shouldn't we think the universe has a designer. Just look at the human eye, it has a specific purpose and so intricately put together to give you sight, does this not need a designer.

John: Yes I can see the argument.

George: Paley then goes on to argue that the regularity of our universe is further proof of the existence of a designer. Our universe is so fine-tuned, so perfectly ordered that this could not have come about by chance. If gravity was slightly stronger the universe would not be able to exist. If the earth was a little closer to the sun humans would not be able to survive. The way the universe, our planet and our lives have come about means this was calculated and planned by an intelligent being which created such regularity for life as we know it to exist. And this being is God. With both Aquinas and Paley's arguments I think it is right to agree that there is an intelligent designer behind the creation of the universe.

John: Although it is a compelling argument I do not think the teleological argument proves the existence of God. There are a lot of problems with this theory.

George: Go ahead, tell me.

John: Well, although I can see Paley's logic; complex watch needs and designer, so complex universe needs a designer; it is still ultimately an argument from analogy. A watch is not the universe it is completely different, so to just infer that the same principles apply by no means proves the existence of God. We have observed a watch being designed and created and so we know if we found a watch it obviously has a designer. However we have made no such observation of the universe so why should we just assume it has a designer.

George: Ok.

John: David Hume said such thought leads you into an anthropomorphic concept of God, as though we have given God human qualities. Look at the reasoning of the teleological argument - a watch is complex so a human designed it, the universe is very complex so a super human must have designed it. This is not really consistent with the concept a perfect God, because a perfect God would be nothing like a human, in any way shape or form so why should we reach the conclusion that just because a human designs complex things God must therefore design even more complex things.

George: So how else would you explain our intricate universe with such regularity? I mean I do not think you appreciate how finely tuned this planet is, how perfectly it is structured.

John: Oh believe me I do, and that is why I think it seems more down to chance than it does an intelligent design.

George: Chance, you think this was all a fluke, all of this such an intricate design, such regularity was just chance?

John: Yes and I think this for two reasons. Firstly, no matter how fine-tuned and regular a universe is it does not instantly rule out the possibility of chance, something I think Aquinas and Paley ruled out too quickly. I understand how precise and accurate the world and the universe had to be in order for life to grow on it, however in an infinite amount of time any possible state of affairs that could happen will eventually come up. So this regularity we see could just be the result of trillions and trillions of years of just randomness, different universes coming in and out of existence and then eventually a universe randomly came about, which resulted in a planet that just so happened to have the right amount of gravity, at the perfect distance from a large star, with the perfect amount of oxygen and a liquid substance enabling life to grow. If we are talking about an infinite amount of time, eventually a planet that can sustain life will come about. Have you heard the theory that if an infinite amount of monkeys randomly hit an infinite amount of typewriters for an infinite amount of years, eventually one of them will randomly type the complete works of Shakespeare word for word. This would not be done through a conscious effort or knowledge by the monkey, it is completely random, however given enough time, the precise sequence of all the letters resulting in Shakespeare's work will randomly get typed. And it is the same with the universe. There may have been billions of universes randomly coming in and out of existence and then finally one that resulted in planet earth with our life. It does not need an intelligent designer to explain such regularity.

George: I don't know if I can agree with that, how can such detail such precise regularity be down to chance.

John: Well that's my second point, why do you think our universe is so great. If you really think about it, you could quite reasonably say that the very planet and universe we live in seems more like chance than design.

George: Really how could you say that?

John: John Stuart Mill's exact words were "Nearly all the things which men are hanged or imprisoned for doing to one another are nature's everyday performances." Meaning nature is cruel, it is violent, we have animals that need to kill other animals for their own survival, we have weather that destroys thousands of creatures, we have diseases that kill all the time, we even have creatures come in and out of existence, animals completely extinct, annihilated , for what reason would this be for. Why would an intelligent designer create such a harsh cruel world? That is so wasteful. If you step back and look at our planet it in fact seems more like something that would come about through chance than through design. The problem is you as a human are so well adapted to your environment, you think it was designed specifically for you, so you are putting in place a designer that you think consciously built this whole planet for you to live on. However we have come a long way in science and Darwin's natural selection and theory of evolution have shown us that humans were not always as we are now, we were animals that changed grew and adapted over time. We look around and think the things around us are here for a specific purpose, but in fact they have just adapted to the environment that they are in. We notice how a bird can fly in the sky, or how a fish can swim under water; this has just been a gradual step by step process over many years which through natural selection has resulted into the beings we see today. As the weak species die the strong species survive changing, adapting and growing to their environment. This planet and this universe was not designed for us, we merely adapted to the environment in order to survive. You think this is fine-tuned by a designer, I am saying this is a random planet come about by chance in a random universe in which over millions of years we have become adapted to.

George: Good point.

The Cosmological Argument

George: We will be finishing off the traditional arguments for the existence of God with the cosmological argument. Now, the cosmological argument is an a posteriori argument that attempts to prove the existence of God. So it is an argument that uses external observations and experiences in order to prove its conclusion.

John: Ok, so how does it prove the existence of God?

George: In short it looks at the functionality of our universe, causation and order. These are things we experience in the universe and essentially these have to come from somewhere, and the argument is that this comes from God.

John: How does it reach that conclusion?

George: There have been many advocates of the Cosmological argument, the most famous was probably St Thomas Aquinas. Aquinas used 5 ways to prove the existence of God, the first 3 are considered part of the Cosmological argument. So let me go through them. The first way is the argument from motion. Everything we see in the universe is changing or it is moving. Now, we know nothing can just change or move by itself unless it has something else that is changing it. If something is dependent on something else for its motion, then how does the whole chain start? Aquinas rejected the idea of infinite regress, the idea that there is not start, that everything is just part of an infinite chain that goes forever into the past, because without a first movement nothing can start the motion off, something needs to begin everything. However if everything needs a mover, and you cannot have infinite regress, then logically you need an unmoved mover, something that moves other things but cannot itself be moved. This we know of as God.

John: Yes the unmoved mover, this was an argument used by Aristotle too.

George: Yes it was. Ok so that is the first way, now the second way is known as the argument from causation. As we can see in our world and in our universe, everything has a cause. Cause and effect, it's the fundamental law of physics. How did the glass fall, I kicked it, I was its cause, who caused me, my parents, who caused my parents, my grandparents and on and on. We can also see that in our universe nothing is the cause of itself, everything needs something beyond itself to be its cause. So then how did the universe come about, what cause the universe, what caused life? Well Aquinas has already rejected infinite regress, we cannot just have an infinite chain of causes, as there would be no first cause to start the chain. So what we need is an uncaused cause, something that does not need a cause, but is responsible for causing everything else in reality. This we know of as God.

John: Yes that makes sense.

George: And finally the third way, also known as the argument from Contingency. Aquinas says everything in the universe is contingent, meaning nothing has necessary existence, everything that exists could not have existed; it is perfectly possible that everything could not have existed. And as everything could not have existed it also means there was a time when everything did not exist. There was a time when the tree down the road did not exist, when the building we are living in did not exist. And it is also important to note that all contingent things rely on something else for their existence. However, if everything at one time did not exist, that means nothing existed, so there was nothing to cause the existence of everything else. So Aquinas agrees there must be a being with necessary existence, a being that was not brought into existence but has always existed and this being we know of as God.

John: Yes I see.

George: So that is pretty much Aquinas' cosmological argument.

John: Well I can see it is a good argument for the existence of God. It uses observational experience to logically prove there is a God.

George: Yes, exactly. So many Philosophers have studied, and redeveloped the cosmological argument and have turned it into a fantastic theory. Leibniz used the Principle of Sufficient Reason to further strengthen the cosmological argument. Leibniz claimed that everything we see in the in world and in the universe has a specific reason as to why it is there and why it exists. As I said, the reason I am here is because of my parents and so on and so on. However we can see everything in our world relies on something else for its existence, nothing is its own reason for existence, but then how can we have a universe if everything relies on something else as its reason. In order for everything to come into existence there must be a necessary being that is the reason for its own existence, and this again is God.

John: Well, although the cosmological argument seems very strong I still think there are a lot of problems with it, and I do not think it conclusively proves the existence of God.

George: Really, like what?

John: Firstly we have no idea how the universe came into existence, no one did and no one will ever experience it. All we are aware of how things within the universe work, but why should we argue that just because the laws that apply within the universe need to apply for the universe as a whole. David Hume raised this objection, he argued there was too much of a big leap within the logic of the cosmological argument. You are basically saying, everything in the universe has a cause, therefore the universe has a cause. This is an assumption, and I do not think you can expect the same laws that apply within the universe to apply for the universe itself.

George: So then how would you explain the existence of the universe without a God?

John: I would agree with Bertrand Russel, in a live BBC Radio debate Russell was debating with Copleston on the cosmological argument, and Russell basically said the universe is just a brute fact, something that exists that does not need an explanation for its existence. Just because everything within the universe has an explanation does not mean the universe needs one. He used the example of the human race and mothers, you have a mother, I have a mother and we are part of the human race. But it seems weird to say the human race has a mother. What applies to the parts within does not apply to the whole. So because everything in the universe has cause, or an explanation or a reason, does not mean the universe has a cause or an explanation or a reason. The universe is just there and that is all

George: Well it seems that is just running away from the issue. I mean to say the universe is just a brute fact and just there seems too simplistic. The universe is not just there, it is contingent there was a time when it was not there. Science has proven this, we have seen with the big bang theory that there was a specific time when the universe came into existence. A point where it was created. So I cannot agree that it is just a brute fact that has always been because it has not always been. It had a start, and for it to have a start means it had a cause. So of course the universe needs an explanation, a reason and a cause because we know it had a cause.

John: No no no, we do not know it had a cause. The big bang theory is accepted by some but it is by no means the conclusive answer. There is other ideas that are gaining recognition like the oscillating universe theory which basically argues in favour in an endless chain of different universes coming in and out of existence. So this universe may have come into existence, but it itself is just part of an infinite chain of universes.

George: So now you are arguing in favour of infinite regress. The idea of an infinite universe.

John: Well yes, I think Aquinas and the cosmological argument rejects infinite regress too quickly, I mean, why should we dismiss infinite regress, on what grounds are you rejecting it?

George: I would like to raise here the Kalam cosmological argument, also put forward by William Lain Craig. This attempts to show the logical absurdity of arguing in favour of an infinite universe.

John: Go ahead.

George: First we need to make a distinction as there are two types of infinite. We have possible infinity and actual infinity. Possible infinity is when something has come into existence at a specific time and will carry on existing forever.

John: Right.

George: Actual infinity is when something never comes into existence but has always existed, it goes infinitely into the past and infinitely into the future.

John: Ok.

George: Now you are arguing in favour of an actual infinite universe. The problem raised by Craig is that if we had an actual infinite universe then it would be logically impossible to ever reach the present time.

John: What do you mean?

George: We reach the present by successive additions. One moment of time is added by another moment of time and then added by another moment of time. But if we have an infinite past, if we could go forever into the past, then there is no point we can begin to add moments in order to reach the present. Think about it, now is the present, we can call this zero, the future moment will be plus one, and the past minus one. If I was to ask you to count all the negative numbers until you reach zero, you never would. There are infinite negative numbers so if you began counting down you will never reach zero. Do you understand?

John: Kind of.

George: Let me put it like this. If you was to set out on a walk to reach a destination, and your destination was an infinite miles away, no matter how long you walked you will never reach it, because however far you walked however many miles you walked, more miles would keep adding on.

John: Yes I understand.

George: This also applies to the past. If the past is infinite, then no matter how much time has passed by you would never reach the present moment. No matter how much time has passed you would always be going through an infinite past.

John: Yes I see.

George: So because of this we have to reject an actual infinite universe and the possibility of infinite regress. The universe therefore needs a beginning point, this beginning point was caused and it was caused by God.

John: Ok one more problem. Why does God not fall with the same problems as an actual infinite universe? Why argue that an actual infinite universe is absurd by still claim God is actually infinite.

George: Because God is not a contingent being, the universe is, the universe is space and time, God is beyond space and time and laws of nature. God is a necessary being so the same absurdities do not apply.

John: Hmmm.

Thomas Aquinas' 5 Ways

George: Now we have covered the three main traditional arguments I would like to look into Thomas Aquinas' 5 ways he attempts to prove the existence of God. These five proofs include the some of the traditional arguments with more theories put forward.

John: Fascinating.

George: Thomas Aquinas was a 13th century theologian and philosopher. He developed the 5 ways or the 5 proofs as sometimes referred, as logical methods of investigation that prove the existence of God. The first 4 ways are seen as versions of the cosmological argument, whereas the 5th way is understood to be a version of the teleological argument. We shall run through each of the 5 proofs now and critically assess them.

John: Let's go.

George: Very well. Let's start with the first and second way. Now both of these follow the cause and effect principle that we all understand. The first proof is known as The Argument from Motion. This argument is heavily inspired by the works of Aristotle within his theory of causation. We can see and understand with our own senses that everything around us is in a constant state of motion, a constant state of change. Everything is always moving, always changing. Leaning on Aristotle's idea of potentiality to actuality, something moves from its potential to fulfil its purpose, what it was meant to do, for example - the seed moves towards becoming a plant, reaching its actuality. However, Aquinas questions, where does this motion come from? Everything is in this state of motion, and for something to move it needs something else to move it, there is nothing that is responsible for its own motion; everything needs a mover. However if everything needs a mover we this will lead to an infinite regress, we will keep on going back and back and back infinitely. Aquinas rejected the idea of an infinite regress and said this is impossible.

John: Why?

George: Well, if we go forever into the past there was no point in which everything started, and with no start how do we have anything. There must be a start, there must be a something that started the motion off, the first cause, the first mover that is itself unmoved. This is known as the unmoved mover, or the Prime mover and this would be God.

John: I see.

George: So, the fact we have a world, and a universe and nature, the fact these are all in a state of motion means it is necessary that there was a being that started the motion off. A being that is not put in motion by another, but the one that creates all the motion in the universe and so this is the first way that proves that God must exist.

John: Right.

George: Then we move onto the second method using the cause and effect principle, this is known as the argument from efficient cause. Now, an efficient cause is something that causes something else. If I build a car I am the efficient cause of the car. The carpenter is the efficient cause of the wooden chair, the builder if the efficient cause of the house.

John: Yes.

George: You can say that your parents are the efficient cause of you, and your grandparents are the efficient cause of your parents and so on and so on.

John: Yes I understand.

George: So Aquinas notices that everything in existence has an efficient cause, if something does not have an efficient cause it would not exist and there is no case in which something is the efficient cause of itself. However if everything has an efficient cause this would lead to an infinite regress as we would keep on going back and back in time, efficient cause preceded by an efficient cause preceded by an so on ad infinitum. Again Aquinas rejects the idea of an infinite regress, logically it does not make sense, infinite regress implies no first cause, and if there is no first cause there will be no sequence to follow and so there would be nothing. But there isn't nothing there is something, in fact a whole universe. So Aquinas claims there must be a first cause, an uncaused cause and this is God.

John: Ok both of these are a very problematic approach.

George: How so?

John: Firstly they fail at their own criteria. Aquinas states that everything needs a mover and everything needs a cause and so the universe needs a mover and a cause, so this must be God. But why doesn't God need a mover. Why doesn't God need a cause? Why is God exempt from this criteria?

George: Because as Aquinas explained God is the first mover. So God is beyond space and time, outside of this realm and so would not follow the same physical rules that apply to what is inside the realm.

John: I think that is an easy escape for the theist. Why should we just accept God is unmoved and uncaused and more so why can't we not use this same reasoning for the universe itself? Can we not say that the universe is uncaused, we can take Bertrand Russel's approach to this and say the universe is just a brute fact, Russell states "I should say that the universe is just there, and that's all." So the universe itself is the uncaused cause, and we can take God out of the equation.

George: I'm sorry but I would disagree here, scientists are in a general agreement that the universe had a beginning, a starting point, known as the big bang. So the universe has not always been there, it had a beginning and so it had a cause, we need something before the universe and this can only be God.

John: No I don't think that is right. Sure I will agree with the big bang but that only explains the beginning of the observable universe, there is nothing to rule out multiple universes, or multiple layers of universes, or perhaps a super universe that all other universes come out of, this causes all other universes and gives all the other universes their motion. This could very well be the first mover of our universe and the uncaused cause of the totality of reality, we do not need to put a God in place.

George: Hmmm well personally I think the existence of God seems more reasonable than the existence of a super universe.

John: Well that is just your opinion. And in fact many would argue that the fixation upon cause and effect is actually quite unreasonable.

George: How so?

John: I would also like to raise David Hume's arguments at this point. Hume claimed that the cause and effect argument for the existence of God actually takes quite a leap. We notice the laws of cause and effect within the universe but why do the laws that govern within, apply to whole. This is just an assumption. Let me give you an example, you can say I have a mother, you have a mother, every human being has a mother but you cannot say the human race has a mother. What applies to the parts does not necessarily apply to the whole. And just because we observe cause and effect within the universe does not mean this applies to the universe itself.

George: I see.

John: And I would also like to raise here that infinite regress is ruled out too quickly by Aquinas. Sure there may seem to be logical problems with this concept, but we are basing this on our empirical understanding of cause and effect.

George: Fair enough.

John: Finally some of us would even argue that a discussion around anything beyond our universe, beyond space and time is meaningless, and this would include arguments for God. Immanuel Kant raised this in his

Critique of Pure Reason, all our knowledge comes from within the physical world, within time and space so we cannot apply what we understand about causation within the confines of space and time to outside of space and time. In short our empirical understanding of causation cannot be reasonably used to prove the existence of a being beyond the empirical universe.

George: Ok let's then move on to the third way. This is known as the argument from Possibility and Necessity. Aquinas made a distinction between contingent beings and necessary beings. A contingent being is something that could not have existed, the non-existence of this thing is entirely possible, where as a necessary being is something that cannot not exist, the non-existence of this being is logically impossible, it must always exist in every possible world. Aquinas then argued that everything in the universe was contingent, everything that does exist could quite easily not have existed, that includes you, me, the chair you are sitting on , the sky above us, everything is contingent. If everything is contingent it also means there was a time where everything did not exist. And if there was a time where everything didn't exist then there would not have been something to create everything we see today. The fact that there exists everything today means there must be at least one thing that is not contingent but in fact has necessary existence in which all contingent beings and things come from. And this would be God. God is a necessary being, who always exists and must always exist, the fact that we have a universe, time, space and matter means the non-existence of God is actually impossible.

John: But again we are running into the same problems, why can't the universe as a whole be considered the necessary thing, why must we put a God in place. In fact why can't we have a sequence of contingent beings going back to infinity?

George: But this would be an infinite regress.

John: Yes but as I have already said, our lack of understanding about the macro reality means we cannot rule out infinite regress, and to many this seems more reasonable than the existence of a conscious all powerful God.

George: Ok, well let's move on to the fourth way. This is known as the argument from gradation. Here we find similarities with Plato's theory of forms. Aquinas argued that we often grade things in terms of good or bad, better or worse etc. There is always a metric in which we judge something. So let's say we see a crowd of people and notice a very tall person, we understand they are tall in comparison to other people of a different smaller height. Likewise we can refer to a good knife this is in comparison to a bad knife, one cuts very well, the other is blunt and does not cut well at all. The fact there are degrees of goodness means there is a standard we are measuring against.

John: Yes I understand.

George: So we say something is cold, in comparison to that which is the coldest, and so there is that which is the biggest, the hottest, the truest, the noblest etc. And so it follows that for there to be great there must be that which is the greatest. There must therefore be something that is perfect that everything is measured against. It is also argued that the maximum in any genus is the cause of all in that genus. And so there must be a perfect in which every kind of perfection comes from and this being is God.

John: This would hold some sort of weight if we didn't have such diverse opinions on what good and great actually are. People always disagree on these things all the time; that is why there are different cultures with different morals. How can we all be measuring against the same standard when we disagree so much in what is good or bad, great or perfect. Surely if God was perfect and we all measure against his perfection we would always and instinctively know what is good or bad, better or worse. This is clearly not the case so I cannot accept the fourth way.

George: So let's move on to the 5th way, this is seen as the teleological argument and is referred to as the Argument from Design. Again we will see similarities with Aristotle's works here. Using the idea of motion, Aquinas argued that all things move towards a specific goal, even non intelligent things, all non-intelligent things in our world have their own purpose, a goal they tend to and follow through natural law. If we take a flower with sun light and water it will grow vertical. We can do this again with a different flower and again the same results. It is this movement, the purpose of the flower following the laws of nature to its end or to its telos.

John: Right

George: Here Aquinas has argued that something without knowledge a non-intelligent thing cannot fulfil a purpose unless it is guided by something with knowledge. Aquinas used the example of an archer and his bow and arrows. The bow and arrow is a non-intelligent thing, its purpose is to shoot an arrow, however without its archer it is just a bit of wood and string it will lay motionless doing nothing. In order for this to achieve its purpose and do what it was meant to do, it needs the archer to place the arrow onto the bow and shoot it. As though in order for the bow and arrow to reach its purpose it needs an intelligent being, someone with knowledge to guide it right.

John: Yes I see.

George: Well then, most of nature is unintelligent, yet nature itself has a purpose, everything within nature is following a direction. So then, if every unintelligent thing needs an intelligent being to guide it, then it seems that nature, our world and our universe needs an intelligent being to give it this direction, to give everything its purpose, and this being is what we call God.

John: Ok but are they really being guided or is this just a random state of affairs?

George: How can this all be random, look at how intricate and complicated our world is, how complicated nature is.

John: Yes but you are saying that because you exist on this planet and have managed to evolve and survive. And so you believe this has been specifically created, tailored to accommodate life, and of course tailored for human beings. But consider for a second how many thousands if not millions of other planets there are just in our galaxy that do not have any life or anything growing on it. If there is such an intelligent creator why is life so scarce? It seems our planet and all life upon it is just be down to luck, a random planet where things behave in a random way, we have just happened to grow and survive on it. There is no guided intelligence to it, just "organized chaos" complete randomness that we have become accustomed to. Life developed and adapted to the environment not the other way around. If this is the case we do not need an intelligent being to guide the non-intelligent things, the non-intelligent things have just randomly come about by chance; we do not need God in the equation.

George: Honestly I think you are downplaying how intricate and complex this planet is for it just to be down to chance.

John: No I am not, if we are dealing with an infinite universe, then eventually a planet that sustains this type of life would have come about, the fact that it is so rare strengthens my point. There would not be millions of planets with life, just the odd one. It is still possible but unlikely and so we have one planet where life has developed and that is earth. Completely down to chance with no designer and no intelligent being guiding nature.

George: Well I suppose we have to disagree on that point.

Descartes - Meditation III
Of God, that He exists

George: One of the most famous philosophical works ever composed was by 17th century philosopher Rene Descartes. The meditations on first philosophy was a deep mental journey Descartes took pondering the nature of our reality, our knowledge and truth. On his quest for truth, the first meditation lead Descartes into a state of doubt, doubting everything that exists, in the second mediation he realised that he does in fact exist and that he is a thinking thing. In the third meditation Descartes carries on the search for truth to see if using the rationalist approach he can discover whether God exists. Descartes begins this thought process by looking into ideas, or to be more precise clear distinct ideas.

John: Ideas?

George: Yes ideas, our thought processes, our mental perceptions. Descartes first divides ideas into three categories, the categories are factitious, adventitious, and innate. Factitious ideas are ones that have solely been created in the mind, let's say a unicorn; imaginary ideas that play no part in reality. Adventitious ideas are ones that appear to come from an external cause, something outside the mind, consider the sensation of heat or hearing a noise.

John: Right.

George: And finally innate ideas, these are ideas that have no external cause and are not created by the mind, but are rather they are there from the start, they are almost put in our minds from the very beginning. They are always true independently of external factors. Mathematics is the example Descartes would give. We have a concept of 1 or 3 or 10, this did not come about by experience it is an a priori truth, mathematical concepts are therefore innate ideas, their truth is not dependent on our senses, they are independent of the world, they are in a sense truths our minds come stocked with.

John: Hmmm.

George: So for Descartes clear and distinct ideas would be innate ideas. Now we have the understanding of how Descartes has categorised ideas and we can move on to the idea of God. Descartes argues that we have a clear and distinct idea of God, he explains this idea as an "infinite substance, eternal, immutable, independent, omniscient, omnipotent, and by which I and all the other things which exist (if it be true that any such exist) have been created and produced." Now this is where Descartes uses the rationalist approach to prove the existence of God. Descartes argues that for him to have this idea of God means this idea must be an innate idea, and for him to have this innate idea it means it would need to have been created by God, and so if God put this idea into the mind of Descartes then that would mean God does exist.

John: Ok this seems like quite a jump, how exactly does Descartes reach this conclusion?

George: Ok, Descartes claims that the idea of an infinite omnipotent being is an idea that he was not the cause of, he did not create this idea of God and this idea did not originate from Descartes.

John: Well why couldn't this idea have originated of Descartes. We are more than capable of coming up with ideas of things that do not exist.

George: Yes possibly, but when we are talking about God we are talking about an infinite being, Descartes argues that as a finite being he would not be capable of creating an idea of an infinite being. Only an infinite being can create the idea of an infinite being, a finite being wouldn't be able to. So the fact that Descartes as a finite being has the idea of an infinite omnipotent God means this idea must be innate, it must have been placed into Descartes' mind by an infinite omnipotent being and so if this is the case it means an infinite omnipotent being needs to exist in order to create the innate idea. This goes to the basics of cause and effect, if the idea of God is the effect then God himself must be the cause and so the degree of reality of the cause must be at least as great as the objective reality of the effect. So the idea of God must have originated from something powerful enough to create it, something infinite, all-knowing, all-powerful. Therefore, God, or some sort of equivalent must in fact exist. Do you see?

John: Well I'm not entirely convinced, is it not fair to say that as a finite being we do not and cannot understand what an infinite being really is, and so we do not possess the idea of an infinite being.

George: Descartes considered this argument but he claimed as he was a finite being and knew he was a finite being, he would only know he is finite if he understood the idea of infinite. If he did not understand the idea of an infinite being he would not understand the idea of a finite being. By knowing that you are finite you therefore understand your polar opposite. And of course Descartes himself could not be an infinite being, none of us could be, as we are currently finite and we would not approach being infinite by degrees.

John: But this seems fairly circular, what Descartes is saying is that we are finite beings, and as finite beings we understand the idea of an infinite being, because we understand the idea of an infinite being the infinite being must have created this idea.

George: Well yes I do not see a contradiction here.

John: Ok here's another objection raised by Thomas Hobbes, do we really have an idea of God. When we have an idea of something be it an angel or a unicorn, we have specific images but these ideas are composed of visible things, be it a small human with wings, or a big horse with a horn. But we do not possess this with the idea God. Sure artists have portrayed God as an old bearded wise human, but really this is not what an infinite being would look like. We have no image we actually have no idea what the image of an infinite omnipotent being would be.

George: This is not really a sufficient objection, ideas are not just in the form of images, we can easily say that feelings such as fear or love are ideas and no such images are represented here, so I would say God falls under this category, God would be an abstract idea an image would not be necessary.

John: I still do not feel entirely satisfied, I cannot accept that just because I have an idea of God this must come from God. I still believe that we can create an idea of an infinite being as finite beings, and so people created the idea of God and his existence is not necessary to explain this idea.

George: Ok fine, let's assume God does not exist, Descartes does in fact do this and starts a line of questioning to see if this is reasonable. Descartes asks, if there was no God what could be the cause of his existence? Descartes now knows that he exists and describes himself as a thinking thing, so then if there was no God how did he come to be. Descartes considers three possibilities. The first one is himself, that he is the creator of his own existence, however Descartes rejects this and we can see why, if you are the creator of yourself you would not have created yourself with such limitations, you would have created yourself perfect, with the best possible life you could imagine. Also, being the creator of your own life would make you somewhat powerful and Descartes is not aware of any extraordinary powers he may possess.

John: Yes I agree.

George: The second possibility would be another source, but not a God, so not an infinite or omnipotent being. Again Descartes rejects this as all that would happen is that it would turn into an infinite regress. The question would be asked what created this source, and then what created that source and so on and so on. Without an infinite source or a God this would go on forever.

John: I see.

George: And finally Descartes considers the possibility that his parents created him. Now of course parents are responsible for the physical creation of their off spring, but this still leads to the infinite regress argument, what created his parents, what created his grandparents etc. So then having rejected all these possibilities Descartes concludes that there must be an infinite being responsible for creating life or thinking things, and this being is God.

John: Well this by no means is a sufficient argument for the existence of God, there are a lot of problems here. We have covered many arguments quite extensively in our Philosophy of Religion debates so I am going to leave this here rather than start another debate on the existence of God.

George: Very well.

Necessary Existence
Reformulation of the Ontological Argument

George: I want to now revisit the ontological argument, looking into a reformulation of the theory with a focus on necessary existence.

John: Interesting

George: The reformulation of the ontological argument was made prominent by the philosophers such as Norman Malcolm and Alvin Plantinga.

John: Ok.

George: I'm going to give a brief overview.

John: Great.

George: If we understand the concept of God to be the greatest possible being that nothing greater can be conceived, then we must therefore agree that God's existence would either be impossible or necessary.

John: Why?

George: Well consider it, if God did not exist then it is safe to say He cannot ever come into existence. The greatest possible being cannot be created or caused at some time, if something else created God this being would be greater and so would contradict our concept of the greatest possible being. So if God does not exist then He cannot ever exist in any possible world and so his existence is impossible.

John: Yes I understand.

George: On the other hand, if God does exist his existence would have to be necessary. If God does exist, He could not have come into existence at a certain time for the same reasons as before, so there wouldn't have been a time where God did not exist. He could not cease to exist for nothing can cause the greatest possible being to cease from existence.

John: Yes.

George: And if you are the greatest possible being you must exist in every possible world. There cannot be a possible where you do not existence. Your existence is part of every possible world. If this is the case then if God does exist, He must always exist in every possible world and so His existence is necessary.

John: Right, so either God's existence is impossible or necessary, but I don't see why we should choose necessary existence over impossibility.

George: Well, if we must choose between impossible or necessary, something should only be considered impossible if the concept is somehow self-contradictory, or logically absurd.

John: Right.

George: If the existence of something is impossible, it means we cannot conceive of a possible world where such a thing would exist. I can use the example of a squared circle, it is safe to say the existence of a squared circle is impossible, and the reason being is that it is a self-contradiction; by definition a circle is not squared and a square is not circular. So I can agree there is no possible world where there exists a squared circle. Can the same be said for God, is God's existence a logical absurdity or a self-contradiction? Most would argue that this is not really the case, and so if there is no contradiction in imagining the existence of God in any possible world, it then means God's existence is not impossible.

John: I see.

George: And so now we can take the further steps to prove the existence of God. If God's existence is not impossible, then we can say there exists a possible world, where God exists. Therefore we have this one possible world where the greatest possible being exists. If there is even one world where the greatest possible being exists it means He would have to exist in every possible world, including our own, because the greatest possible being must have necessary existence. There cannot be a possible world where this being does not exist as it would cease to be the greatest possible being. And so, if God's existence is not impossible it means we can conceive of a possible world where He exists. If we can conceive of a possible world where He exists, it means He exists in every possible world as He has necessary existence, and so this reformulation of the ontological argument goes the distance in proving the existence of God.

John: Very interesting, this version of the ontological argument sure does sound convincing however, there are still many problems with this theory.

George: What?

John: The reformulation of the ontological argument has only demonstrated that the existence of the greatest possible being can be possible, but the same logic can also be used to show that the existence of a perfect being is impossible. I would like to raise Peter Van Inwagen's concept of a 'knowno'. A 'knowno' is a being who knows there is no perfect being; so a being that somehow knows there is no God. Now, there is no reason to believe that the existence of a 'knowno' is intrinsically impossible, it is not a self-contradiction or a logical absurdity. If then we accept that a 'knowno' is not intrinsically impossible then we also must accept that there is a possible world where a 'knowno' exists. If there is a possible world where a 'knowno' exists then this means in that possible world there does not exist a perfect being, yet a perfect being has to have necessary existence and so should exist in every possible world, if it lacks existence in one possible world it does not have necessary existence and so it is not a perfect being. If then we accept the existence of a 'knowno' we must accept that the existence of a perfect being is impossible, and if we accept the existence of a perfect being we must accept the impossibility of a 'knowno'.

George: Hmmm.

John: As we can see, there is no reason to accept the existence of either a perfect being or a knowno, the problem is that only one can exist and so we have no good reason to accept one over the other. It is because of this I shall argue that the reformulation of the ontological argument is unsuccessful in proving the existence of a perfect being.

George: Good point.

Leibniz: Best of all Possible Worlds

George: Let us now return to the problem of evil and look into the works of the philosopher Gottfried Leibniz and his best possible world argument as a solution to the problem of evil.

John: Great.

George: As we have already discussed, the traditional Judeo/Christian belief in God is that God is a being that possesses omnipotence, omniscience and benevolence, meaning God is all powerful, all knowing and all loving. Of course when we see all the horrible aspects of our world we would naturally question these attributes. Think of all the disasters that take place, all the wars and killings, diseases and plagues all the suffering and pain we humans have to endure. Why is this the case, surely if God is all knowing He would be aware of how much evil and suffering there is on this planet, surely if God was all powerful He would be able to stop it all and surely if God was all loving He would want to put an end to human suffering, so then why does it still exist, why do we have to deal with so much anguish and evil in this world? And thus we have the problem evil. How can evil and an all-powerful loving God both exist. This problem has always troubled theists, Leibniz however believed he had found the solution to this problem and introduced the best possible world argument, we are now going to look further into this and see if it does solve the problem of evil.

John: Great let's begin.

George: Very well. So using a syllogism, we can frame the best possible world argument as such.

Premise 1: God is omnipotent omniscient and benevolent.
Premise 2: God could have created any universe to exist.
Premise 3: Because God is omniscient he would know which would be the best possible universe to create.
Premise 4: Because God is benevolent he would want to create the best possible world and universe.
Premise 5: God created this existing world in this existing universe
Conclusion: Therefore this is the best possible world that could exist

…So the world we have is the best possible world that God could have created, out of all the possible worlds that God could have brought into existence this is the best possible one, and so God is still omnipotent because an all-powerful being can only do that which is logically possible, and God is still benevolent as he still chose to create the best world possible. So whenever we see or experience any type of suffering and question our faith we must remember that this world is the best world that could have existed, the best world that a benevolent omnipotent, omniscient being could create, the best possible world that could be. If reality was any other way it would only be worse; this theory has also been labelled as Leibnizian Optimism as it is adopting the optimistic position that we live in the greatest possible universe and we should be happy we have a loving God that wants us to live in the best reality and has created the best possible reality for us.

John: Ok I feel there are a lot of philosophical problems with this theory and I have quite a few criticisms here.

George: Right, well let's hear them.

John: Let me first start by questioning if the greatest possible world is actually logically possible. I feel like if God thinks of all the possible universes he would never reach the greatest possible universe as this would be infinite. It is like asking what the largest possible number. This cannot logically be achieved. So any world that can be thought of, we could just think of something to make it better, and then something to make that world better and something to make that world better and so on and so on ad infinitum. Basically, I do not think it is logically possible to conceive of the greatest possible world and so not even an omnipotent being could then create the greatest possible world.

George: So, Leibniz does actually address this point using the principle of sufficient reason. The principle of sufficient reason states that for anything that exists there is a reason for its existence. Now, if there was no best possible world then God would have no reason to create one world over another, what reason would there be to choose between two subpar or imperfect worlds, how would you choose which to create. So if there was no best possible world then no world or universe would have been created. But a universe has been created which means that God must have known this was the best possible world and so He would have had reason to create this universe and this world and this reality as we know it.

John: Ok so let's assume if a benevolent omnipotent God does exist they would want to create the best possible world, do you really think this is the best of all possible worlds. You even said yourself, think of all the disasters there are, all the violence, the wars, think of all the plagues famine diseases natural disasters. How could this possibly be the best possible world, if you step back at look it at you can really make a pessimistic case that this is a dreadful world, maybe one of the worst possible worlds there could be.

George: I think you are misunderstanding what Leibniz means by best possible world, it does not mean a world with no pain or suffering or evil, where everyone is happy, it means just the best world that is logically and physically possible to make, Leibniz is not saying that the best possible world would have no evil, he is saying that the evil and suffering we have now is part of what the best possible world would look like. And so you may see certain horrible parts of this world, but as Leibniz says an imperfection in the part may be required for a perfection in the whole. Imagine finding one piece of a puzzle and it looks ugly, but when you slot it in with the rest the end results is a beautiful picture.

John: But we are not talking about a small imperfection here we are talking about hundreds of thousands of years of human suffering.

George: Yes but again it is part of the best possible world. You can make a case that this evil is necessary in experiencing good; that pain is needed for pleasure, that disaster is needed for courage to exist, that murder is needed for free will to exist, that evil is needed for good to exist. This all is the balance of the universe and the best possible world that God could have created. You also have to remember how much beauty and joy there is in this world, how much love and pleasure. This has all been created for us to experience too, evil is just a necessary component of this majestic greatest possible world.

John: Ok let's just ask this. Could we not say that just one child less dying of starvation would make this world a bit better? Just one child less. This would not impact the grand scale of the design, it will be one less child dying and so it would result in a slightly better world. If you agree with this then you agree this is not the best possible world.

George: But that's the point, we cannot know if that is the case, perhaps in another possible if that one child does not die it actually results in more evil in some way. We cannot know because we do not have infinite minds and we do not have omniscience, but God would know this and so that one child would need to starve in order for this to be the best possible world. If there was a better world possible, a world with less child starvation a world with less disease, if this better world was possible then God would have brought this about. Alas we have the world we have and so this and only this has to be the best possible world.

John: I still cannot accept this. This feels like the theist is just running away from the argument, simply claiming God works in mysterious ways, or telling me that I cannot understand Gods reasons for the misery around me is not an adequate response. I feel an omnibenevolent God would be able to create a far, far better world than the one we have. I see no logical contradiction in eliminating famine and plagues and considering that a better world. I see no logical contradiction in only creating good natured humans that might have the option of doing evil but chose not to. If anything, when we look at how horrible this world can be, it further strengthens the argument that this is in no way the best possible world. The simplest feeble minds can conceive of a better world. If you are therefore standing by the principle of sufficient reason and accept the devastating world we live in it would strengthen the argument that God is not omnipotent, omniscient or benevolent or in fact it would strengthen the atheists belief that there is no God.

George: Hmmm interesting.

The Omnipotence Paradox

George: I want to go back to the nature of God and look at a paradox that arises known as the omnipotence paradox.

John: Interesting.

George: As we have established, within the main monotheistic religions God is believed to be omnipotent, meaning He is all powerful. God, the creator of the heavens and the universe, the creator of all life, is an all-powerful being. There is nothing that God cannot do. God is seen to have unlimited powers, He is an infinite being. However with omnipotence comes a very tricky problem and that is known as the omnipotence paradox. We will discuss this paradox and look into potential solutions.

John: Great let's get started.

George: Ok, so essentially the omnipotence paradox highlights the contradictory nature of omnipotence itself. The most popular way this is framed is with the very simple question. Can God create a stone so heavy that He cannot lift it? If the answer is no then this puts limitations on God, as He is therefore unable to create something, how can an all-powerful being not be able to create something. The fact that He cannot do something means He is not omnipotent. If however the answer is yes, God can create this stone, then hypothetically it would mean that there would be this stone that God is unable to lift, God would not have the power to lift this stone and so this would be something else He cannot do, further limiting his power and so showing that He is not all powerful. So either God cannot create the stone, or God can create the stone but He cannot lift it. Either way this simple question shows the utter contradiction in the existence of omnipotence.

John: I see.

George: Such a contradiction means that omnipotence is just not logically possible. No being can therefore be omnipotent, this then casts doubt on our traditional belief in the nature of God and also casts doubt on God Himself.

John: Yes I see the paradox, however I do believe the theist can escape this problem and still maintain a belief in an omnipotent God.

George: How so?

John: It can be argued that although omnipotence means all powerful, the power only extends to the logically possible. An omnipotent being cannot be expected to have the power to do the logically impossible.

George: I am not sure what you mean.

John: For example, an omnipotent being cannot be expected to create a square circle, because by the very definition a squared circle is a logical contradiction. A circle cannot be a square and a square cannot be a circle, by definition. You cannot expect an omnipotent being to create something that is soaking wet and completely dry at the same time, an omnipotent being cannot create a window that is both opened and closed at the same time. These are logical contradictions. All powerful means having the power to do anything that is logically possible, it does not mean the being can do the logically impossible.

George: Ok, assuming for one second that is true, I do not see how God creating a rock so heavy He cannot lift is a logical contradiction. I understand that a squared circle or an open closed window is, but I do not see how a rock too heavy for God to lift is in itself a logical contradiction.

John: Because it does contradict God's very nature. If you have an omnipotent being then by definition you cannot have something that is greater than it. God is all powerful, and God is infinite, to then have a stone that God cannot lift means somehow this stone is greater than God, it is bigger than the infinite, heavier than the strongest being that can exist, greater than that which nothing greater can exist, as Anselm would say. So by definition this is a contradiction. You cannot have something bigger than the infinite, greater than the greatest possible being. The existence of the stone would contradict the nature of God, so logically the stone cannot exist, the existence of the stone is a logical contradiction, and God cannot do the logically impossible. So God cannot create the stone, but not because He is not omnipotent God cannot create this stone because He is omnipotent.

George: Ok but I want to challenge the idea that an omnipotent being cannot do the logically impossible. Why must we accept this premise?

John: Because of the law of non-contradiction. Contradictory premises or statements cannot be true at the same time. I am human and I am not human cannot both be true, as they contradict each other. So either God is omnipotent or the infinitely heavy stone exists they cannot both exist, and if one accepts the omnipotence of God then the omnipotence paradox is not a problem as it goes against the law of non-contradiction.

George: But where does this law come from?

John: What do you mean?

George: The law of non-contradiction, where does it come from? Where do any logical laws come from, where does logic itself come from?

John: I am not sure I understand your point.

George: Think about this, God is seen as creator of everything right. The creator of the universe, of all the laws of nature.

John: Yes.

George: Then surely God is the creator of logic and all logical laws. The omnipotent being would have created the laws of logic, the omnipotent being would have created the law of non-contradiction. So for you to say that God cannot commit a logical contradiction, that God cannot create a square circle means you are saying that God is bound by logical laws, God must follow these, He cannot break or change them. So here we have another dilemma, similar to the Euthyphro dilemma. If God is bound by the laws of logic, it seems almost that they existed prior to God, God did not create them, they were already in existence and they are eternal, and God must follow them and His powers are only possible within this logical scope. This would imply that God is not the creator of everything, that the laws of logic are in fact greater than God and so would call into question His omnipotence. If however you agree that the laws of logic was something created by God, all logical rules and laws were designed and implemented by this omnipotent being, then we must expect this omnipotent being to be able to commit logical contradictions and so the omnipotence paradox still remains as a problem and this again calls into question his omnipotence.

John: Ok fine, so I will then accept the second point of your logical Euthyphro dilemma. God is the creator of all logical laws, as an omnipotent being God therefore sits outside the laws of logic. So the question is asked, "Can God create a stone so heavy he cannot lift?" The answer would therefore be yes and no. It is impossible and so it is possible. God cannot do it and He can do it. God has never done it yet He does it every day. This stone exists and it does not exist. If logic is something that only humans follow then we cannot expect God to follow it, and we cannot be expected to understand a being that is beyond logical laws as our minds can only function within the scope of logical laws. So calling into question God's omnipotence or existence with logical paradoxes is pointless and meaningless.

George: Very interesting point.

Pantheism

George: I want to finish off the nature and existence discussion with a slightly different take on God than the traditional Judeo-Christian belief, nonetheless a very interesting theory, so let's discuss the theological theory of Pantheism.

John: Fascinating.

George: Now, pantheism is a very unique approach to theism within the philosophy of religion. To give a brief summary; pantheism is the belief that God is in fact the universe. A pantheist rejects the idea of a transcendent God, a pantheist rejects the belief that God is something separate from the universe, that God is something above and beyond the cosmos. Rather, God and the universe are the same thing, the universe is God, the two are identical, everything around us, the totality of reality is the divine, God is everything and everything is God.

John: I see.

George: Now the typical monotheistic religions see God as a personal God, by personal we mean a God that has personhood, has its own identity, speaks in the first person, shows emotion. A personal God is often depicted in an anthropomorphic way, given human like qualities, not just in looks, but in personality too, we hear of God's love, God's wrath, God's mercy etc.

John: Yes.

George: Pantheism completely stands against this concept, whilst Pantheism is a theistic belief or some may refer to it as a deistic belief, God is not seen in a personal way, rather, the very reality we are in, everything we see, the deep dark empty corners of the universe this is God.

John: Interesting.

George: Pantheism has been around for many many years, it can be said to have been included in a number of religions and mythologies over the years, it was in fact made prominent in the west by the philosopher Baruch Spinoza among many others. Now, pantheism itself is quite a broad belief system, encompassing many different beliefs and theories within the one overarching doctrine. The purpose of this video is to give a broad look at the strengths of pantheism as a spiritual belief as well as look at some of the philosophical problems that arise within this branch of theism.

John: Great.

George: Ok, I would like to propose 3 main arguments that show Pantheism as the most logical and valid form of theism for one to adopt. The first is the classical religious approach, the second the personal or individual approach, and the third is the scientific approach.

John: Ok.

George: Starting with the classical religious approach. In traditional theism God is described as being omnipresent, God is everywhere at all times. Now, really, how can one distinguish from God being omnipresent in our reality to God actually being all of reality? What exactly is the difference? To say that God is everywhere all the time is to say that God *is* everywhere *all* the time, God *is* everything. This is then the pantheist approach. More so, classical theism adopts God as omniscient, meaning God knows everything, He has knowledge of the past the present and future simultaneously, again this is a type of temporal omnipresence, being all of time all at once. Again this is pretty much identical to the pantheist approach, if God is reality then God is time, God is the whole cosmos at every moment past present and future. A very rational development to the classical theist approach.

John: Very interesting.

George: Also the classical theists will often claim that the universe is dependent on the existence of God, God has to exist for the universe to exist, making the universe a part of God, basically synonymous. The logical next step is to equate the two, if God must exist for the universe to exist then the universe does not seem like something separate from God but in fact seems part of God, leading to the pantheistic approach.

John: Yes I understand.

George: Moving on to the personal or individual approach, many people often have a numinous experience by just seeing or experience parts of reality. It happens when we see a beautiful view of nature, or a magnificent site of the stars, we can feel it when we embrace the love of another person, or even in a deep state of meditation. Many people say that they have felt God, or maybe just felt an extraordinary feeling. This experience is like an awareness of being part of something greater, and what better way to explain it than the simple fact that we are part of something greater, we are part of God. God is all of us, and everything else. We are all part of the same infinite entity.

John: Yes I see.

George: And finally the scientific approach. The trouble with any traditional theology is that God is seen as being outside the universe, beyond space and time. Science then has no place in the affirmation or discovery of such a being as science is solely the study of the empirical and observable universe. Any talk outside of human experience can be seen as redundant, however, should we agree that God is the universe itself, we can now inject meaning into the discussion.

John: Right.

George: So on a cosmic level, should we see the universe or perhaps the multiverse as actually infinite, something that has always existed, did not come into existence and will not cease to exist, can create matter ex nihilo and is responsible for all the laws of nature; then this definition of the universe seems identical to the traditional belief in God and we have good grounds to view the two as identical.

John: Very interesting, you have raised some great points as to why pantheism seems a reasonable and perhaps logical approach to theism. It almost functions as a great middle point between religion, spirituality and science.

George: Yes exactly.

John: However I want to now look at some philosophical problems with this theistic approach.

George: Very well.

John: Focusing first on the classical religious approach, I do not really see a different between pantheism and atheism.

George: What do you mean?

John: Pantheism rejects a personal God, so does atheism. Pantheism rejects an anthropomorphic God, so does atheism. Pantheism accepts the physical universe and only the physical universe, so does atheism. So where exactly is the difference. Schopenhauer claimed that "Pantheism is only a euphemism for atheism," and "to call the world God is not to explain it; it is only to enrich our language with a superfluous synonym for the word". I am inclined to agree. An atheist rejects God as the creator of the universe, they just accept that the universe exists, the pantheist has the exact same line of thought, but has just renamed the universe to God, this is a linguistic difference and nothing more. There is nothing that separates God from everything else in our universe, so why even make the distinction. Pantheism and atheism ultimately remain the same thing.

George: I don't think this is necessarily true. Atheism is the rejection of God, Pantheism is saying that God is the universe.

John: Well I do not see what the difference is.

George: I believe the difference will come down to consciousness, for the universe to be God, means that the universe needs to possess a type of consciousness. Atheism would reject any form of consciousness outside a physical living body, whereas pantheism can reach out to consciousness as a way to bolden the theistic element of the belief.

John: So according to the pantheists the universe has consciousness. The universe itself has its own thoughts and feelings?

George: Not in a personal way with its own identity, not like how a classical personal God is described, but rather on a higher level.

John: I am not sure I understand.

George: Ok firstly let me reiterate that pantheism encompasses a wide set of beliefs so there will be differentiations. However a popular pantheistic approach to the universe's consciousness comes under the Panpsychism approach.

John: What is panpsychism?

George: So panpsychism is the idea that consciousness, or you can say mind-like qualities, exist everywhere in the universe, in all things all the time, however there are different levels and degrees of consciousness. The tiniest most fundamental element of matter, right down to the subatomic level, also known as monads, will contain conscious qualities, however these monads will vary in degrees of conscious strength. How conscious something is depends on how complex the entity is and how many strong conscious monads the entity contains. So an inanimate object like a rock will have very weak conscious monads, a plant slightly increasing in complexity will contain slightly stronger conscious monads, an insect a more complex organism will then have slightly stronger conscious monads, an animal even stronger conscious monads, and a human will of course have very strong conscious monads. This does make perfect sense as we can see varying degrees of consciousness and sentience throughout our natural world. We can even go so far as to say humans themselves contain varying degrees of conscious monads, giving rise to the existence of super geniuses.

John: Right.

George: Now the universe as a whole, the most complex and greatest entity contains the total sum of all monads that exist, as well as the power to create these monads, which would make the universe the highest form of consciousness possible. Again this is exactly how we understand the classical concept of God, but we are breaking it down to a more empirical understanding. God is therefore the total sum of all consciousness in the universe, it is not sperate from the universe, it *is* the universe, but it obtains a greater level of consciousness which means pantheism is vastly differentiated from atheism.

John: Ok, but this idea of monads still seems like a wild belief.

George: Perhaps but I would say they are a physical belief rather than a metaphysical belief, and something we can hope for science to answer one day

John: Very well but from here we run into the problems for your personal approach.

George: How so?

John: If our consciousness is just part of a bigger complex entity, then how is it we have developed our own personhood with our own identity. I feel like my own person, my own thoughts, my own feelings, my own beliefs, my own emotions. I do not feel like my consciousness is part of anything else, or is joined to anything else. I do not feel like my mind is a small part of a greater mind.

George: But how would you know if it was?

John: Would we not be able to share conscious experiences, to be more mentally linked and mentally synced?

George: Perhaps but that is by no means self-evident.

John: But surely this idea will undermine the concept of personhood. And if we are all part of this hive mind does that imply that I do not think for myself, that my thoughts are somehow controlled by this supreme consciousness.

George: I suppose you can do what you will but you cannot will what you want.

John: Then this causes huge problems for the ideas of free will, as well as personal identity.

George: I agree but I do not think this is grounds to dismiss the theory. Also if you claim, as you do, that you have this complex consciousness, and you are undoubtedly part of the universe, then how can a part be more complex than the whole? Surely if you possess this complexity then the totality would be infinitely more complex.

John: Hmmm.

George: Great point.

Chapter II

Religious Ethics

Thomas Aquinas' Natural Law

George: Let's now look into religious ethics and focus on the Aquinas' theory of natural law.

John: Right.

George: The central idea behind natural law is that human beings have an innate power to understand good and evil. God has written moral law into nature and He has created all humans with the ability to know what morality is and to recognize what is good and what is evil.

John: I see, so why does Aquinas advocate the natural law theory.**George**: Good question. Aquinas got most of the grounding for natural law through the works of Aristotle. Aristotle believed that everything in nature was constantly changing and moving, and this movement was all towards its specific purpose, or telos as Aristotle referred to it.

John: Yes.

George: Well, Aquinas agreed with this, he agreed that God created the world in this goal driven manner, where everything was following strict natural laws to fulfil its specific purpose.

John: Ok.

George: Aquinas said this was the same for humans. Human beings are themselves moving to their telos, he refers to Aristotle's concept of Eudaimonia, you could say it is like a heaven, or a state of bliss, true and pure happiness. So Aquinas believed Eudaimonia was only achieved in the afterlife, but it did not stop humans pursuing this and moving towards it, and we move towards Eudaimonia by pursuing what is good and avoiding what is evil. If we as humans always strive to pursue good and avoid evil we get closer and closer to our purpose and to reaching Eudaimonia.

John: Ok well there's a bit of a problem here. Aquinas says we reach Eudaimonia by pursuing good, but how exactly do we know what good is?

George: Aquinas argued that this is through human reason. Human beings have the unique capability to reason, to be self-aware, to think and understand their surroundings and their lives. This reason will unlock for us our moral knowledge, and we will be able to recognize good and we will know how we should live, we will know how we should act.

John: Right I see.

George: Now, Aquinas went further, he argued that when we use our reason we notice basic goods that all reasonable humans pursue. The main purposes of life, what near enough all humans want and what all humans are drawn towards. He distinguished 5 basic goods that he referred to as primary precepts. The primary precepts include…

- Life: So the preservation and promotion of life.
- Reproduction: So the continuation of the human race.
- Education: This more so education of one's offspring, so they will know how to continue the human race, live better lives and even protect you when you get old.

- Worshiping God: Aquinas saw how we innately seek God, we try to understand and make sense of our life as a whole.
- And finally law and order: This promotes justice, and allows us to live in a functional well maintained society where humans can grow develop and be safe.

John: I see

George: So these are the primary precepts, the basic goods. Aquinas then goes onto to say that natural law continues from the primary precepts into the secondary precepts. Once our reason acknowledges the primary precepts we use our reason further to derive our rules, laws and behaviour in accordance with the basic goods. So the specific laws, or behavioural codes are the secondary precepts.

John: I am not sure I understand.

George: Ok well let's take the first primary precept of life, the promotion of life. Our reason has acknowledges this is a basic good to follow. We then think about murder, as murder is taking a life, it goes against the primary precept of promoting and preserving life and so it goes against natural law. So murder is something we shouldn't do, murder is wrong. This would be a secondary precept.

John: I see.

George: Or if we take school, school is a place where children go to learn and become educated. Educating your offspring is a primary precept, school is something that follows the primary precept and therefore follows the natural law, school is therefore good; this is another secondary precept.

John: Yes, yes I understand.

George: So this is the fundamental theory of natural law. Morality is an absolute God given natural law, that all humans have the innate ability to discover by using our reason.

John: This does seem like an interesting theory on human ethics. However a lot of problems can be raised.

George: Like what?

John: Well, if morality is a natural law God has written this into nature, and all humans have the innate ability to reason and discover these laws then why do people violate the natural law? Throughout all of human history, all the time, humans have violated the natural law, murder, theft and other horrible crimes. Why, if all humans possess an innate ability to understand morality, is there so much immorality?

George: That is a good argument. Firstly we need to understand that natural law for ethics is not like any other natural law. I can't violate the law of gravity for example. However for moral law we need to remember that God is balancing this with free will, so it is necessary that I am physically able to violate moral natural law.

John: Yes ok but why would anyone want to.

George: This can be down to human emotion. We are at the end of the day emotional beings, we do not live by just reason alone, and so sometimes our emotions can get the better of us, it can cloud our reason and lead us to do wrong things and violate the natural law. When we break a basic good our reason is being overpowered by emotion and we do things that we deep down know we shouldn't, but that's exactly it, our reason has been pushed deep down.

John: Ok, here is another issue I have, you would agree that natural law is an absolutist theory. As morality has been written into nature it must be absolute.

George: Yes correct. What is good and what is evil is absolute, it is not dependent on an outcome but God has created this as a law, an action is within itself either right or wrong.

John: So how would natural law deal with moral dilemmas, where violating a natural law would actually bring about more good?

George: What do you mean?

John: Well consider someone who must commit a morally bad action in order to fulfil a morally good action. Let's imagine we are in a hospital and there has been a power cut, the backup generator does not have a lot of power. In the emergency room we have 3 people who need urgent care or they will die. In the room next door we have a man in a coma on a life support machine, with no signs of recovery. As the backup generator is weak, the only way we would save the three people in the emergency room is to unplug the life support machine and use the power. So what are the choices; if we do not unplug the life support machine we let three people will die. If we do unplug the support machine, we are actively killing someone and so violating the natural law of life.

George: I see. Aquinas had a response to this. He refers to the Doctrine of Double Effect. When faced with dilemmas like this we need to look at the situation and ask - was the action one wanted to do good, and was evil intended in the action. So with regards to the hospital example, we want to save the three people, is this good, yes I would say it is, this is still preserving and protecting life. So when we unplugged the life support machine did we intend evil, not really, our intention was to save the three people which is good, we did not intend to kill the man in a coma, this is not what we set out to do, it was just an unfortunate situation, but the intention was always good. So what we done was morally good, it just had a bad side effect, so this means it is permissible under moral law.

John: This seems problematic, how can this be an absolutist theory. How can morality be absolute if natural law can be violated when we deem necessary.

George: We're talking about situations in which the intended action is good, the unintended side effects are violating the natural laws, we however, as agents, are not intending to violate the natural laws but rather promote them.

John: This is just casuistry, you can bend and shape and violate the natural law depending on what we think will generate the most good. This feels more like a consequentialist theory than an absolutist one.

George: I see.

John: And finally, what good is the natural law theory if you do not believe in God. You can argue that God has created natural law for humans, and that our moral laws are created within nature. But if we reject the whole concept of God, and deny He exists then where does that leave natural law, as the whole theory relies on God. This theory can only appeal to religious people, no one else really has a reason to adopt this.

George: Good point.

The Euthyphro Dilemma
Problem for Divine Command Theory

George: Sticking with religious ethics I want to now revisit the Euthyphro dilemma and discuss how this is a major problem for the Divine Command Theory.

John: Interesting.

George: To give a brief summary of the divine command theory, ultimately it is the idea that morality comes from God, what is good is that which is commanded by God, and what is evil is that which God forbids. We learn about morality through the divine or religious texts, such as the Bible the Torah the Quran etc. By reading and understanding the religious texts, a moral person is the one who follows the rules of God.

John: Understood.

George: However, within the divine command theory there arises a dilemma known as the Euthyphro dilemma. Originally written by Plato as a dialogue between Socrates and Euthyphro, it was then studied by many religious and ethical scholars, to put it simply the Euthyphro Dilemma questions the nature of divine command theory and leads to two fundamental points about morality coming from the divine.

- Points 1: Is that which is morally good, good, because God commands it.
    … Or …
- Point 2: Does God command it because it is morally good.

John: Please explain the dilemma again?

George: Well let's look into. Would you agree that that which is morally good is good because God commands it?

John: Yes I would agree with that statement.

George: So you would agree that God is the creator of morality, if God commands something it is automatically morally good because God has commanded it, and if God forbids something then it is automatically morally wrong because God has forbidden it. Morality is completely and solely down to what God wants.

John: Yes I agree.

George: So here lies the problem, in this case morality becomes completely arbitrary, there is no morality other than that which God decides, no universal moral laws, right and wrong, good and evil are just down to how God feels. Morality is not then based on any reason, or wisdom or rationality but just on how God feels, and this could change moment to moment.

John: I see.

George: Suppose one day God comes down from heaven and visits you, God then commands you to kill innocent people for no reason other than for his personal amusement, if you agree with the first point of the Euthyphro dilemma you have to agree that killing innocent people is morally is right because God has commanded it. So as I said morality becomes arbitrary, not concrete and so not really real.

John: Yes I understand, ok so in that case I would have to side with the second point, I would say God commands something because it is good, so morality is real and concrete and God commands us to live in a moral way.

George: Ok so let's look at the problems that arise with this. If God commands something because it is good, God has not in fact decided what is good, He just knows what is good.

John: Right.

George: But this then implies morality is something over and above God, something not created by God and cannot even be controlled by God, morality is in fact something God discovered, something God is bound to. God recommends good, not because He has decided this, but because this is the right and moral way to live.

John: I see.

George: All of this poses a huge problem for God's omnipotence. If God did not create morality, and is bound by morality, He therefore cannot change morality, God cannot command what is evil and make it good, this limits Gods power and his omnipotence.

John: Yes.

George: Morality then does not even need God to exist, if God commands something because it is morally good, then we can take God out of the equation and what is morally good still exists and still applies to us.

John: Right.

George: And so this is the main problem with the second point, ultimately if morality is over and above God then God is not the law giver, jus the law discoverer, morality is bigger than God and something God must follow.

John: Interesting.

George: So there we have the Euthyphro dilemma. If that which is morally good, is good, because God commands it, then morality is just down to the whims and fancies of God, it becomes fluid and arbitrary. And if God commands what is morally good because it is morally good, then morality becomes something over and above God, something God is bound to and cannot change therefore limiting his omnipotence.

John: Fascinating dilemma and indeed a huge problem for Divine Command theory.

Chapter III

Religious Meaning and Belief

Religious Language

George: Let's now focus on some of the wider religious concepts and discuss on a philosophical level. We'll start with religious language and we'll be asking the question - does religious language have any meaning?

John: Interesting.

George: Now let's take religious statements, such as "God exists" or "God is omnipotent" or "God is love", we must ask ourselves, do these statements have any meaning or are they in fact meaningless statements?

John: I would say meaningless statements.

George: Why?

John: Let's define what we mean by meaningful and meaningless statements. A meaningful statement is a cognitive one, it is one that is subject to cognition and is either true or false.

George: Right.

John: A meaningless statement is one that is not true or false, there is no factual knowledge associated with the statement, as the statement cannot be verified.

George: Yes.

John: Here is where I would agree with ideas of the Logical Positivists, in particular A.J Ayer. He claimed a statement can only be meaningful if it can meet the verification principle. The verification principle states that meaningful statements are those that are synthetic, so they can be empirically verifiable. Or they are analytic, true by definition. So if I say a triangle has three sides, this is meaningful as it is true by definition. And also if I say it is raining outside, this is a meaningful statement, because we can empirically prove if that statement is true or false, we can actually go outside and verify if it is raining or not.

George: Yes I understand.

John: Now, any religious statement, any statement about God is a metaphysical statement and Ayer would argue they would all be meaningless statements, because they cannot be empirically verified. You say to me God exists, but how can I verify that statement, it is not possible for me to verify that statement, I cannot show you that the statement is true, I cannot show you that the statement is false. That statement is therefore not true or false it is just a meaningless statement. You saying God exists is the same as saying blah blah blah; it means nothing as it adds nothing to our lives. It fails the verification principle. And for this reason I would argue religious language has no meaning.

George: Ok I understand what you are saying, but where would you stand on statements that can in theory be verified but not in practise?

John: What do you mean?

George: If I was to say there is a little green alien sleeping on the dark side of the moon, is that a meaningless statement, as we cannot now go to the moon and verify it.

John: Yes but the criteria of verifiability allows for statements that we know how to verify even if we cannot verify them at this precise time. So I know how to verify the alien statement, I would need to take a rocket to the moon and look to see if there is an alien sleeping there. We know how to verify that statement so it is not a meaningless statement.

George: Well I would argue that religious statements can then in theory be verified.

John: Really?

George: Yes. John Hick used the example of the Celestial City, a metaphor for heaven. Two people are walking along the road trying to reach the city, one of them believes they will reach it, the other does not believe it exists, but when they turn the last corner they will know if this city exists. So we will all eventually find out if God exists or not. Once we die either we go to an afterlife and verify God's existence or we do not and we find out God does not exist.

John: I'm sorry but I do not agree with this. Any verification of God will need to come from outside the empirical world, we are looking at meaningful language within the empirical world, using empirical facts to verify our statements. Needing to rely on an afterlife as a means of verification is not sufficient to give meaning to religious language.

George: Hmmm.

John: And also, if there is no afterlife you are dead, and you are not able to verify that God does not exist, so I do not think this is a good argument.

George: Ok but still the verification principle has a fundamental flaw.

John: What is that?

George: It fails at its own criteria

John: What do you mean?

George: Well the verification principle says that a statement is only meaningful if it is an analytic statement or synthetic statement, but that actual statement is neither analytic or synthetic, it is therefore meaningless. So the verification principles entire criteria is a meaningless statement, it fails by its own standards.

John: I see.

George: So I cannot see how you can claim religious language has no meaning, if by the very criteria you use to determine this, would also have no meaning.

John: Good point, but I still stand by the position that religious language is meaningless, and I think the Falsification Principle best explains this.

George: What is the falsification principle?

John: The falsification principle was developed by Karl Popper as part of the philosophy of Science. Popper claimed that scientific knowledge was gained once a hypothesis was made and a scientist would test this and would know under what circumstances the hypothesis could be falsified. If a scientist knew what they needed to see in order to agree their hypothesis would be rendered false, then this was meaningful.

George: I see.

John: So if a scientist made the hypothesis that water boils at 100 degrees celsius, they would know that if they saw water boil at less than 100 degrees this would falsify the hypothesis. The fact that the scientist knows what would falsify the hypothesis gives the statements meaning.

George: Yes I understand.

John: Now, Anthony Flew took this approach and used it for religious language. Flew claimed that if there was absolutely no situation in which a religious person would abandon their beliefs as false then any religious statement was meaningless.

George: I am not sure I understand.

John: Ok, Flew gave an example of a gardener. Two people stumble across a patch of land with some flowers and bushes. One of the people thinks this looks lovely and says this land must have a gardener. The other person disagrees; so the two decided to verify whether there is a gardener. They put cameras near the garden to try and catch the gardener, when the camera showed no signs of a gardener, the person who believes claimed that this gardener must be invisible. So they put motion detectors on the ground to sense if someone walked there. When the motion detectors did not buzz, the person who believed said the gardener floated above the ground. No matter what was done, for the believer, there was nothing that could falsify the belief in the gardener.

George: I see.

John: This is the same with religious people. They say God exists, is all powerful and all loving. I say, but we have never seen God, they say that it is because he is invisible, I say but there is so much evil in the world, they say God works in mysterious ways. There is no evidence to ever falsify their belief in God. So the falsification principle would say, if you are not willing under any circumstance to accept the falsification of your belief then all your religious language is meaningless. If a theory is unfalsifiable it cannot be proven true or false and so remains meaningless.

George: Ok I understand your point but you seem to only be basing meaning upon statements that meet a scientific standard, this is not self-evident. You have just started from this position, not all statements must be empirically verified or falsified for them to have meaning, this is only true of scientific statements, but there are more types of statements than just scientific ones. You are judging the meaning of all language statements with a scientific criteria.

John: How else can you give meaning to something?

George: Well R.M Hare would have agreed that religious language cannot be shown to be true or false however it does not mean that it is meaningless. Hare coined the term Blik, a Blik was something that influences how one views the world and is not necessarily based on fact or reason. A Blik changes their perception of the word, the way they live the way they act etc. So these are in fact very meaningful even if they do not fall into the sphere of empirical science. So being religious is a Blik, it affects many things in a person's life, their beliefs on morality, their belief in an afterlife, the friends they choose, the partners they choose, how they socialise. These things are all important and all stem from religious language so religious language must have a lot of meaning as it shapes people's lives. It does not need to meet the empirically verifiable scientific method in order to have meaning.

John: I am still struggling with this. Ultimately religious language is neither true nor false, how can one take meaning in a statement that cannot be verified or falsified, it might as well be strange noises.

George: Again you fail to venture outside of the scientific realm, language is a lot deeper than this. Wittgenstein in fact argued that language functions in a similar way to games. Just like each game has its own set of rules, so too does language, and meaning comes from understanding which language game we are playing. So if we use the word field, when discussing academics the word field refers to a specific subject someone is studying. But when talking about sports, the word field refers to the grass area the game will take place.

John: I see.

George: So language has different meaning in different circumstances and meaning is dependent on the context that words are used. We need to figure out which language game we are playing to determine the meaning. In a language game of science I would agree religious statements have no meaning, but in a language game of spirituality then religious language would have a lot of meaning. Just like using the rules of tennis in a game of football, I believe you fail to see the meaning of religious language as you are stuck in the science language game.

John: Interesting.

Religious Experiences

George: Let's now look at religious experiences and ask, if the fact that religious experiences have been reported does it in fact help prove the existence of God?

John: Interesting.

George: So throughout history and through all different religions people have reported religious experiences, both religious and non-religious people alike. I want to first look at how exactly we define what a religious experience is, and what makes it religious as oppose to any other experience.

John: Ok.

George: Now the term religious experience seems quite broad, at first one may just think it is any experience that involves a type of religion, so praying or going to church.

John: Yes.

George: When debating religious experiences in philosophy this isn't exactly what we mean, it is actually more profound than this. One of the best definitions comes from the philosopher and psychologist William James, he defines a religious experience as "the feelings, acts and experiences of individual men, so far as they apprehend themselves to stand in relation to whatever they may consider the divine".

John: I see.

George: So it is effectively an experience where you are in the presence of the supernatural or the divine, this experience can come as a vision, as voices, or even just a feeling, but ultimately the experience will bring one closer to God. James went on to explain that there were in fact a four characteristics of a religious experience. One was that the experience was ineffable, it could not simply be explained or be put into words. Number 2 was that the experience was noetic, meaning one would receive knowledge from the experience that is otherwise not available through human experience. The third is that the experience would be transient, meaning it is short lived, it is a short experience. And finally the experience would be passive, the person is not in control but in fact the experience was being completely controlled by a superior power or by God.

John: Right that makes sense.

George: Following the works of William James, the theologian and philosopher Richard Swinburne developed a further explanation of a religious experience and explained there were five types of religious experiences. One is public ordinary experience, this is when one will experience something that exists in public that is completely ordinary, like someone seeing a sunset, a starry sky or a beautiful landscape, yet they feel this is the work of God, they believe they are looking into the creation of a superpower and this feeling has religious significance.

John: Right

George: The second is public extraordinary, this is when one sees something in public that in fact violates the natural laws, so witnessing a miracle, if for example you're at the beach and witness the parting of the sea, this would be a public extraordinary experience. The third is private describable, so a completely private experience you had, no one other than you can feel, see or hear this experience, yet you are able to exactly explain this experience in normal language. The fourth is private non-describable, so this would again be a private experience but you cannot explain this in normal language, you might only be able to give metaphorical explanations. And finally a nonspecific experience, this is like a constant feeling that God is there, you can feel a supernatural or a superior power present and always around.

John: Interesting.

George: And this last point by Swinburne is similar to the descriptions from Rudolph Otto who described religious experiences as a numinous experience, by numinous Otto meant as a feeling of being in the presence of something greater, feeling a sense of awe as you can feel you are around something so big, so powerful and so much greater than you.

John: Ok good, I think I have a sufficient understanding of what constitutes a religious experience.

George: Brilliant, ok so let me ask you, with so many people reporting to have had a religious experience do you think this in fact is proof of the existence of God.

John: No I do not.

George: Why?

John: I am just going to be honest and say that I do not really believe anyone who claims they have had a religious experience. When I hear stories of people who have had visions of angels, or heard the voice of prophets or felt the presence of God, I just do not believe them. I believe they are either mistaken, exaggerating, confusing a normal experience for a religious experience or just plain lying. Either way, the fact that I do not believe a religious experience has ever or can ever occur means for me it does not prove the existence of God.

George: See I think you are being unfair to religious experiences. If I say to you that this morning I saw a pigeon flying in the sky you wouldn't even consider that I was lying or mistaken. You would automatically accept what I have said and believe me. Yet as soon as people claim they have a religious experience you they are met with automatic scepticism and disbelief.

John: Well yes and there is a very simple reason, I have seen a pigeon fly in the sky, many times, it is an experience I am accustomed to. If you said to me the pigeon flew down and spoke to you then I wouldn't believe you because I have never experienced this. Likewise if you say you saw an angel or Jesus in a vision I wouldn't believe you because this is nothing I have experienced before, this is a supernatural experience, so I have no reason to believe in the supernatural if all I have experienced is the natural.

George: Ok but nonetheless, just because you have not experienced something does not mean it cannot or has not happened. You would be pretty ignorant to only believe in the things you have experienced. Many people experience many things in the world that you have not. Swinburne raised this argument and called it The Principle of Credulity, we should in fact believe what people say unless we have proof that what we are being told is false. We should not approach what people say thinking it's false and asking for it to be proven true, but the other way around, we believe it is true until we can prove it is false. Swinburne also raised The Principle of Testimony, Swinburne argues that by in large people do tell the truth, and so we should believe their experiences unless we know for a fact that what they are saying is false.

John: I am sorry but I completely disagree with the two principles. I know that people are often mistaken, people often believe what they want to be true rather than what is, and people often lie, either for attention or fame or whatever. Swinburne's principles would near enough accept any story unless you can prove it is false, however it is virtually impossible to prove a negative, the burden of proof lies on the person making the claim, not on the person denying its validity. Look, If I said to you, whenever I am alone, and there are no cameras or recording equipment the teddies in my room come alive; how could you possibly prove what I am saying is false. It's too difficult to prove a negative, so I start from a basis of incredulity when what I hear goes against my understanding of the natural world. And as such I do not believe anyone has genuinely had a mystical or religious experience, and so do not believe this supports the existence of God.

George: So you think everyone who has had a religious experience is lying.

John: Not necessarily, some are, some may have been hallucinating due to being intoxicated on drugs and alcohol, some may just be confusing an ordinary experience with a religious experience. Like they asked for God help then heard a thunder storm, and suddenly felt a strange feeling. This can be confused as a numinous experience but really it was a weather coincidence that got you over excited.

George: Hmmm.

John: Freud raised a similar argument. He believed that religious experiences were essentially illusions. You have to understand that religious thoughts or beliefs are deeply rooted in our psyche, even in certain atheists. It is a large part of our culture, and can play a major role in people's upbringings. So when one has a so called religious experience they are essentially projecting their inner most beliefs desires and even fears, it is a product of human psychology, Freud says it is like a childlike longing for a father with need for protection against the consequences of his human weakness, I would maybe argue it is a desire to be close to the creator, to understand life and where we come from, and help us understand who we are. Maybe if we have a religious experience it will prove we are not just empty matter floating through infinity on a giant ball, but maybe we are a little more special. But this is ultimately wish fulfilment, we want it to be true, so we convince ourselves it is true when really the religious experience was nothing more than an illusion, and does not support the existence of God any more than the experience of seeing the pigeon flying in the sky.

George: Good point but still it makes me wonder. So many reported cases of religious experiences, so many people saying they have had them, even corporate religious experiences, groups of people all at the same time. I don't know if I can comfortably argue every single person had an illusion

John: Well until it happens to me I can't believe in them.

George: Well there you go.

<u>Miracles</u>

George: I think now is a great time to focus on Miracles. We may understand a miracle to be a violation of a law of nature, it's an event that cannot be explained by natural or scientific law, and this event is often attributed to a supernatural cause, this is usually described as coming from God. A common example of a miracle would be Jesus Christ coming back from the dead, or Moses parting the red sea. Something that does not naturally happen, but can only happen through divine intervention.

John: Yes exactly. Within most religions miracles have been reported and the followers of these religions will hold that God does perform miracles and can violate the laws of nature at any time.

George: Right, so I ask you, do you believe in miracles, or in fact, do you believe a miracle can happen?

John: Well no, I don't.

George: Why?

John: In short I do not think we have enough evidence to support the existence of miracles. I agree with David Hume's take on the subject. Hume did not believe a miracle could occur, he argued that a miracle had never been "attested for by sufficient number of men" and most reported miracles have come from among ignorant and barbarous nations. What Hume means by this is that a miracle has never been witnessed by a large number of people all at one time. Rather when a miracle is reported it is often by one or two people. And most reported miracles have come from time periods of little scientific discovery and knowledge about the empirical world. And don't forget people want to believe in miracles, they want to believe that their God exists and can intervene, Hume claims this want, is what leads to a sensible tendency towards a belief in miracles. So of course there will be hearsay, exaggerated stories and gossip, which will lead to outrageous claims of miracles but this does not lead me to believe that there is a God who can break the laws of nature.

George: Well, two points I want to address, you mentioned that miracles have not been attested for by a significant number of men, I think this is not a good argument by Hume. I mean what does Hume define as a sufficient a number? Does it need to be 5 people, 10 people, what's is the criteria? Secondly, regarding the ignorant barbarous nations, how do you define what constitutes an ignorant barbarous nation. Many people in the modern age have reported miracles. I do not see how these points are enough to be believe that a miracle cannot happen.

John: Ok, if miracles do exist how comes so many different religions have claimed to have witnessed a miracle? Think about it, each religion claims to be the true word of God, but if there can be only one true word of God, and therefore only one true religion, how can all religions claim a miracle has occurred. If a miracle was to occur in ancient Rome this would show that Roman Gods exist, however then we hear of miracles in the Christian religion and this would show that a Christian God exists and so on and so on. It is because of this one would be compelled to disregard miracles all together as their existence is used by too many different people at different times.

George: Again this isn't really a good enough argument. When a Christian or a Hindu or any other religion claim to witness a miracle it is not meant to support any specific details of the religion it is just meant to show that there is a God. Different religions can witness miracles by the same God I do not see a contradiction with that.

John: Well let me raise another point by David Hume. He claimed that as the concept of a miracle is a violation in a law of nature, by its very definition it should not ever be able to take place. Laws of nature are a strict set of laws and regulations which govern our earth. They cannot be violated under any circumstances as this would defy the entire concept of a law of nature. They are said to be regular and constant so any sort of violation or change would break this regularity. Because of this I cannot believe that a law of nature can be violated, and so I do not believe a miracle could occur.

George: I would not agree that is a good enough argument against the existence of miracles. Richard Swinburne argued that although laws of nature are regular and constant, they can still be broken. This would be rare, and can only be done by an omnipotent creator, but there is no contradiction arguing that we have laws of nature created by God and occasionally the all-powerful creator can break his own rules. Just because the law of nature can be broken by God does not mean the whole law must be suspended.

John: Interesting, so let's think about this then. What if, when one claims to have witnessed a miracle, they have not in fact witnessed a violation in a law of nature, but just an extremely rare occurrence that is very much part of the existing law.

George: What do you mean?

John: Let's say we are standing around in a park one day and all of a sudden you start floating in the air. Now, I look at this and because of my knowledge of gravity as a law of nature I see this as a violation and I scream, "miracle".

George: Ok.

John: Based on what we know as the law of gravity we believe this is a violation to the law. However, what if the law has not been violated. What if the actual law of gravity is that it persists all over the world for 10 million years at a time, and every 10 million years, in that specific park it ceases for a few seconds. This is very much part of the law of gravity, this is how it works, it's just a very very rare occasion that no humans have ever witnessed before, or will witness again. So, me floating in the air is therefore not a miracle, just a rare occurrence within a law of nature.

George: I see.

John: So then, can we not say that all reported miracles, if they are true, were not actually violations of laws of nature, but rather extremely rare circumstances that are still perfectly natural. And so if they are perfectly natural events then they are not in fact miracles. With our recent take on quantum physics, scientists appreciate that the universe may not be governed by a constant set of rules, but laws of nature are more fluid, which would lead to miraculous events just being part of our everyday universe.

George: I do not think I can agree with that. If something so unusual was to take place, something which has never happened before, it would seem absurd to just believe that it is a perfectly natural event, it's absurd to think that our whole understanding of a law of nature would need to be changed to allow for this one never seen before event.

John: You think that is more absurd than believing an all mighty God caused a violation in the laws of nature?

George: Well yes.

John: Ok well let me ask you, why would an omnipotent creator need to break a law of nature. Assuming there is a God if he is all powerful why would He ever need to create a miracle? Surely He could engineer life the right way without the need to get involved? God having to get involved and cause a miracle seems like He is going out of his way to correct a mistake. But how can an omnipotent being even create a mistake?

George: Hmmm.

John: And also, as miracles are rare, it seems God only intervenes occasionally, Maurice Wiles raised this point. Judging by the current belief in miracles it seems God cares about some people more than others, and that is why only very few people witness miracles while the vast majority are not so lucky. That does not seem very nice. One person claims there life was saved by a miracle, and yet so many others die everyday. Why does this person get the miracle but no one else?

George: Right.

John: Why did God not intervene during any of the devastating wars we have had, or in any of the atrocities humans have had to endure. As Wiles said, even though miracles are rare by nature it seems strange that nothing prevented Auschwitz or Hiroshima. Perhaps God is just lazy and only intervenes sometimes but usually He does not care much about the world. Either way this all does not seem like the same omnipotent and benevolent God that you claim causes these miracles.

George: Good point, of course we would never be able to understand why God does anything so can we really judge.

Pascal's Wager Argument

George: We will now focus on an argument for the belief in God and that is Blaise Pascal's Wager argument.

John: Great.

George: Pascal was a 17th Century philosopher and mathematician who gave a compelling argument as to why we should all believe in God. Now, please note this is not an argument that attempts to prove the existence of God such as the ontological, teleological or cosmological argument. This is not even an argument that attempts to show the existence of God as more likely than not, Pascal is not trying to prove God's existence, Pascal is only trying to show people that we should in fact believe in God; and we have good reason to do so.

John: Ok how does Pascal do this?

George: Pascal developed the Wager Argument, this is effectively the gambling persons approach to a belief in God.

John: Interesting.

George: So, Pascal effectively adopts Decision Theory, this is the study of ones choices and outcomes and the formula for the best decisions, this is often used in gambling, for any gambling situation decision theory will weigh up the chances of winning with the value of the winnings, and decide based on this. So if we have a lottery with a jack pot of $1 Billion, with 1,000 tickets available at $1 a ticket, the odds of winning are 1000 - 1, but we stand to win $1billion at the risk of only $1; decision theory will say gambling $1 is a great decision.

John: Yes.

George: Pascal adopts this approach for the belief in God and turns this into a gamble, looking at Decision Theory this is how Pascal has approached the situation:

- Either God exists or God does not exist and we have to either believe in God or not believe in God.
- If God does exist and we believe in Him we will be rewarded with an eternity of bliss in heaven.
- If God does not exist and we believe in Him, nothing has changed in our lives and this does not affect us.
- If God does not exist and we do not believe in Him, nothing has changed in our lives and this does not affect us.
- However if God does exist and we do not believe in Him we will be eternally punished, an infinite amount of pain and suffering in hell.

For a gambling man, and using decision theory we would clearly see that believing in God is the best decision. By believing in God we risk nothing but stand to gain an infinite amount of happiness, whereas not believing in God, we gain nothing but we risk everything and infinite amount of pain. As Pascal Says "Let us weigh the gain and the loss in wagering that God is... If you gain, you gain all; if you lose, you lose nothing. Wager, then, without hesitation that He is." So whether God does exist or not, whether this can be proven or not it doesn't really matter, the absolute best decision we can make is to believe in God, and so this is wager we should make, thus it becomes Pascal's wager argument, the gamblers approach to philosophy of religion.

John: Fascinating argument but instantly I have an objection.

George: What's that?

John: You mentioned that believing in God and God not existing involved no loss, here I would disagree I do in fact think there is a loss. Think about it, focusing now on the Judeo-Christian religion, for you to believe in God means you will need to attend church every Sunday, you cannot have pre-marital relations, you cannot cohabit, there a restrictions and rules on a lot of your life, you must live your life in fear constantly trying to appease and please your Deity. This is not easy and this takes away quite a bit of your freedom and your personhood. Now to go through all of this for no God, to live a religious life where a God does not exist I would say is a huge loss, we only really get one life and you can potentially waste it down a religious path for no reason. This needs to be considered in decision theory and factored into the Wager.

George: Yes I understand what you are saying and there are two responses to that point. Firstly you can indeed factor it in to the wager and there will be a small finite loss considered on the "Believe in God but God does not exist" category, it's not a huge loss because a religious life is not necessarily one of immense physical pain, and it is finite because it is only for the duration of your life. However when we compare this to, "do not Believe in God but God does exist" category you are weighing this up to immense physical pain for an infinite amount of time, essentially an eternity in hell. So this is still outweighed and it still looks like the better decision is to Believe in God.

John: I see.

George: The second point, and what Pascal would most likely argue is that a religious life is not a negative thing and carries no real loss. A religious life puts value in things like community, family, it gives people purpose and also eliminated the fear of death with a promise of eternal paradise. So believing in God carries no loss, and if God does not exist it does not really matter as your life have been better off with just the belief.

John: Hmmm, well I'm not sure about that, this is probably more of a subjective opinion.

George: Either way, to believe in God still seems the more intelligent gamble.

John: Ok but how exactly can you believe in God if you don't believe in God. Is belief a choice, I would not say so. I think you just believe or you don't. Sure something can happen that makes you change your beliefs, but just saying to someone believe because it is a better gamble seems strange and something that is impossible to do. If you have learnt about the concept of God, and seen no real evidence to convince you how could you possibly force yourself to believe in Him. And if you are just pretending to believe in God this is not a genuine belief this is an inauthentic belief in God. So you can go through the motions so to speak, you go to church, you read the bible, you follow the rules, but you don't truly believe in your heart of hearts that He exists, you have some doubt; then if God does exist and he is omniscient, He will know. He will know you have been faking your belief for your own selfish reasons and that cannot possibly end in a reward.

George: Good point.

John: Also what Pascal has not factored into the wager is other religions. There are so many different religions with different beliefs in different Gods. If you choose the wrong religion and worship the wrong God you run the risk of ending up in an eternity of pain, this needs to be factored in, and when it is, the choice does not become so clear cut.

George: Yes I see.

John: But the most pressing objection is that really, this has not added any evidence to the existence of God, it has given us no reason to believe in God other than to have our backs covered, but this argument can be used for absolutely everything. I can say to you I believe in Hades, the Lord of the underworld, once you die if you do not believe in Hades he will take your soul to the underworld for eternal damnation, so following Pascal's wager you should also believe in Hades. Do you now believe in Hades?

George: Well no.

John: Exactly, it can be used for any metaphysical or supernatural being and after a while it will be redundant we will believe in absolutely every possible deity or demon even if they contradict each other.

George: Good point.

Russell's Teapot

George: We have covered arguments for the existence of God and for the belief in God, now let's look into an interesting analogical argument against the belief in the existence of God known as Russell's Teapot.

John: Great.

George: Now, Russell's teapot is a hypothetical argument the purpose of which is to show that in debates one cannot be reasonably expected to prove a negative, rather it should always be on the person making any sort of claim to prove their point. Russell's main focus of the teapot argument was aimed towards Religious believers and their unfalsifiable beliefs.

John: Ok so how does Russell illustrate this?

George: So, imagine if someone comes to you and claims that – "between the Earth and Mars there is a china teapot revolving around the sun in an orbit." That's right, there is a teapot floating in space. What would you say?

John: I would ask for proof of this teapot.

George: And suppose this person then says that "the teapot is too small to be detected by telescopes or satellites, there is no way we can see this teapot, but it is definitely there", how would you respond?

John: I would ask why this person has come to this belief.

George: And suppose their response is "because it cannot be disproven, there is no empirical way to disprove the existence of the flying teapot", would you then believe in this flying teapot.

John: No I wouldn't.

George: Why?

John: Because no evidence for its existence has been displayed.

George: Ah but there is no evidence for its nonexistence either, you have no proof that this teapot does not exist.

John: That doesn't matter, their belief is solely relying on not being able to disprove it; that in no way proves it exists. Not being able to disprove something is not evidence of its existence.

George: Exactly, and this is Russell's point, unfalsifiable claims do not mean they are true or real and it gives us no reason to adopt them. Saying to someone, you cannot disprove X, gives us no good reason to actually adopt X. If someone claims something exists, it is not enough that the claim cannot be falsified, it is necessary that the claim is verified. Arguing that one's beliefs need to be disproven is also known as the burden of proof fallacy.

John: Yes I understand.

George: So Russell's main aim for the argument was towards religious beliefs. If someone came to you and said, there exists an all-powerful being who knows everything, created the whole universe and human life, you would surely ask for proof, some sort of evidence to back up the claim. If they in turn respond by asking you to offer disproof, or rather to prove the negative, to prove that God does not exist, this is equivalent of them asking you to disprove the existence of the floating teapot. It is nonsense and a fallacious argument. The burden of proof lies on the one who makes the claim, it is the responsibility of the person with the belief to prove their belief, the sceptic cannot be expected to prove the non-existence of their belief and it is fallacious to expect someone to prove a negative. Unless evidence can be displayed all unfalsifiable beliefs are just as meaningless as a belief in a flying teapot.

John: Yes indeed, however I would like to challenge Russel's teapot.

George: How?

John: I am not going to argue against the burden of proof fallacy, however I would like to spin this analogy in favour of the theist.

George: Go ahead.

John: Suppose we are walking in a vast field in the British country side. After miles and miles of complete empty land we stumble upon a brick built house, a really lovely house, double glazed windows, a chimney, a lovely front door etc. I then turn to you and ask – "how do you think this house got here?" How would you respond?

George: Well I would obviously say builders were once here and they built this house.

John: Ok, and if I then said to you, "no, I do not believe builders were here, I believe builders were never here, in fact no conscious being has ever visited this land, this house just appeared out of nothing, all the bricks, and glass and wood, just came into existence out nothing and arranged itself into this house." What would you say to that?

George: I would think you were talking nonsense.

John: Right, but what if I then said to you that you could not in fact disprove my claim. There was no evidence that shows my belief is wrong, there is nothing disproving that the house came into existence out of nothing.

George: Well then I would say you are falling into the burden of proof fallacy.

John: Exactly, because of your understanding of the empirical world, because of your understanding of cause and effect, you claim the burden of proof should be on me to prove that this whole house came into existence out of nothing. So then, when the atheist makes the same claim about the entire universe is it not fair that they too should share the same burden of proof. If the atheist can claim that the whole universe, all the planets, the stars, all matter all conscious minds, came out of nothing, no creator no designer then why do they not share this burden of proof, why does the atheist not have to justify this magical nothingness that somehow spawned an infinite reality, the same way a theist must justify this magical being that created this infinite reality.

George: Hmmm very good point.

Chapter IV

Religion and Existentialism

Nietzsche – Nihilism and the Ubermensch

George: In this discussion we will turn our attention to of the most famous Philosophers of the 19th Century, Friedrich Nietzsche.

John: Interesting.

George: Nietzsche is seen as one of the pioneers of Nihilism, as well as a major contributor to the existentialist movement in Philosophy during the 20th Century. In this video we are going to look at how Nietzsche reached a nihilist position, and his ideas on the Ubermensch.

John: Great.

George: First we need to understand a little history. Since the great Roman Empire, Europe was a Christian continent. Nearly all people followed the Judeo Christian teachings, on the creation of the universe, the creation of the human race and of course morality.

John: Right.

George: However during the 19th Century there was a huge cultural shift sweeping across Europe. The development of the natural sciences and the works of Darwin caste doubt across the whole Judeo-Christian religion. People were in fact losing their faith and losing their religion. Nietzsche, picking up on this cultural shift, declared that "God is dead". He explained… "God is dead. God remains dead. And we have killed him. How shall we comfort ourselves, the murderers of all murderers?"

John: Wow, very dark.

George: Yes but this perfectly summed up the state Europe was in during the enlightenment. Imagine that for centuries people strongly believed in one God that created them, they believed they were created for a reason, that the Earth was the centre of the universe and they had been placed on this planet by an omnipotent being. This gave all people a sense of purpose. No matter how rich or poor, how strong or weak, or how beautiful or ugly, we had all been created by the same God for a specific purpose, and we are all governed by the same moral law and judged all the same. And no matter what, we are all equal in front of God and we are all either rewarded or punished in the afterlife.

John: Yes.

George: But as science developed and we understood more about human evolution suddenly the stories in the bible did not seem true. Religion was declining, and soon God was dead. But with the death of God it left a huge void in the lives of millions. Suddenly we were not important, we were not the centre of universe, we no longer had a purpose, morality meant absolutely nothing, there was no God to judge right and wrong and judge our lives. There was no afterlife for reward or punishment. No purpose, no reason no creator and no morality. Life was empty, life was meaningless, this was the birth of nihilism.

John: Wow.

George: Now this a lot to take on, morality is now pointless, values are meaningless, everything we would have valued means nothing; truth, honesty, loyalty all these are no longer virtues, but just mean nothing.

John: So where does Nietzsche go from here?

George: Well, Nietzsche agreed that with the death of God this void will inevitably lead to Nihilism, however he believed there was a way to fill this void and bring some sort of purpose or meaning back to life. Nihilism was not the end result but humanity had something to strive for.

John: What was that?

George: In his book Thus Spoke Zarathustra, Nietzsche raised the concept of The Ubermensch.

John: Ok what does that mean?

George: The Ubermensch, literal translation is the Super Man, or some refer to it as The Overman. Now that God is dead and we realise we are all alone in the universe we need something to take the role of God, so Nietzsche thought this was up to mankind, we must strive for our own evolution, the next phase of man, the more superior better man, the super man.

John: I see.

George: Consider our evolution, our ancestors were apes, now how far more evolved have we become, and yet why should we assume our evolution will stop. We need to carry on getting better and we must aim to either create or become an Ubermensch. For Nietzsche this was the goal for humanity.

John: Ok what exactly defines an Ubermensch?

George: Nietzsche wasn't exact on this but there were some core ideas he had to the concept of the Ubermensch. Firstly, the Ubermensch is psychologically strong, ready to master this life and this world. The Ubermensch is not concerned with other worldliness, the only concern is for this world, this life and everything in it. Nietzsche saw religious systems such as Christianity solely concerned with other worldliness, the idea of heaven, and eternal reward, this other worldly fulfilment would pull people away from this world; it will make them distant from our earth and concerned with a world that they did not live in. The Ubermensch would be solely focused on this world the Ubermensch will grasp this reality and appreciate it.

John: I see.

George: But most importantly the Ubermensch will rise above all morality and values that were once ubiquitous and establish his own values. The Ubermensch will create his own morality, it will be based on this life that he has lead, the experiences that he has had. The Ubermensch will not be controlled by herd mentality; following the morality of the masses because they have been told what is right and wrong. The Ubermensch creates morality for themselves, they define what should be valued, they live by their own moral code. The Ubermensch brings their own meaning to a meaningless world. The Ubermensch dominates their reality.

John: Hmmm interesting.

George: So this is the goal for mankind, we do not need God to bring meaning to our lives, we find meaning by striving to become the Superman.

John: I find this fascinating I truly do, and I can see how this would lead an atheist or an agnostic away from Nihilism. Yet I can't help but find some problems with the concept of the Ubermensch.

George: Really?

John: Yes.

George: Like what?

John: Well it seems Nietzsche has not spelt out specifically or in great depth what makes an Ubermensch, but we have some vague ideas on self-mastery, being psychologically strong and defining our own morality. However if we are not currently supermen, and do not know of any such being ever existing, then how could we possibly know what an Ubermensch would be. Nietzsche is trying to explain a higher evolved human, but how can a lesser evolved human, who has never come into contact with an Ubermensch, know what one would be like. So what really is an Ubermensch? Is this a guess, is it a fantasy, or perhaps nothing more than Nietzsche's personal opinion of what a super human would be?

George: Yes I see.

John: A further criticism would be if an Ubermensch can in fact define their own morality, how would this work in a world with over 7 billion people. Let's assume we all reach the ultimate goal and the whole of humanity has become an Ubermensch, we all share this world, so if each person has their own morality and values then I think it will inevitably lead to clashes, two different moralities that are inconsistence with each other. How could such a world function and how could it be resolved if two Ubermenches contradict each other?

George: Well I would like to think that if we all reach the stage of being an Ubermensch then all our morals and values would sync, we would all be on the same wavelength and there would not be any inconsistencies or contradictions

John: Really, you think this? How could 7 billion people each create their own morals yet each follow the same morals?

George: Because they are all higher beings, they are all super men so will have a better grasp of morality.

John: But think about what you are saying here, you are referring to morality as an objective thing, something that exists beyond people, and something we can discover and get closer to. This is exactly what Nietzsche rejected, morality was not objective or universal; this was something the herd believed. Objective morality died with God so I find what you're saying hugely contradictory.

George: Hmmm, good point.

John: If God is dead there cannot be objective meaning, the choices are nihilism or subjective meaning. But with subjective meaning we cannot expect universal meaning that is the same for everyone.

George: Yes I understand.

John: Also, going back to the idea that God is dead, don't you think this is a bit of a leap?

George: What do you mean?

John: I understand discoveries in science showed parts of the bible and parts of religion as inaccurate, but to go from that to God is dead seems quite drastic. It can be argued that one can agree that parts of the bible are inaccurate but not the whole of the bible. It could be argued that religions outside of the monotheistic religions could be true. It could be argued that sacred texts are meant to be read and understood metaphorically rather than literally. But most of all and what I would argue, religion and God are not synonymous, you do not have to accept religion to accept God. And whilst holes have been poked in the bible I do not see how you reach the conclusion that God is dead. The concept of God is greater than any religion, you can disregard religion but still keep hold of a belief in God. So just because science has developed it does not mean that God is dead.

George: Good point.

Kierkegaard - Three Stages of Life

George: Continuing with the existentialist movement I want to now look into the works of Soren Kierkegaard, often regarded as the father of existentialism he also developed what can be considered religious existentialism and so I think it is worth discussing within the philosophy of religion.

John: Great.

George: One of Kierkegaard's most famous works was his idea on the three stages of life. Kierkegaard claimed that in order for one to develop into their true self they must pass through the three stages of life. These stages were the Aesthetic, the Ethical and finally the Religious. Once an individual has passed through these stages they have become complete, they are true and they are aware.

John: Interesting, so what exactly is involved in each stage?

George: Ok, starting with aesthetic, we understand aesthetics to be concerned with art and beauty, but Kierkegaard characterised the aesthetic stage as being solely focused on sense experience, the aesthetic stage for the individual is immersing themselves in pleasure, it is a type of hedonism, looking for anything that will cure ones boredom, to bring excitement and delight into their lives. But at the same time it is self-serving, it is devoid of any deeper meaning. In the aesthetic stage the individual only cares about themselves and maximising their sensory pleasure, they do not acknowledge a community, and their role in something larger than themselves. All individuals must go through the aesthetic stage but you should never remain in this stage indefinitely, life is greater than hedonistic pleasures and an individual needs to be concerned with more than just themselves.

John: Right.

George: So one must then move onto stage 2, the ethical.

John: What is involved in stage 2?

George: This is where the individual sees himself as part of something bigger than himself, the individual will start to see himself as part of a community and start understanding the social norms. It's called the ethical because in stage 2 an individual becomes aware of good and evil, they develop personal responsibility as well as a commitment and responsibility to others. This can be characterised as having a spouse, children, co-workers, people who rely on you. In stage 2 you have risen above a concern for just yourself and your pleasures, but you are now a part of a bigger community, and there are bigger principles or social norms that you are now submitting to. Your motivations are more than your sensory desires and appetites, the ethical makes one's life bigger and more meaningful.

John: Ok, and then what's the 3rd stage.

George: So, the 3rd and final stage to becoming your true self is the religious stage. Ultimately this is understanding that we are all a small part in the infinite creation of God, and the religious stage is to develop complete and utter faith in the existence of God. Once an individual has found this faith they have reached the 3rd stage, religion is therefore the highest stage in human existence.

John: Ok so what religion is Kierkegaard advocating for? I am assuming Christianity given the time period and country he was born in.

George: Yes but not exactly. For Kierkegaard, religion was the awareness of a metaphysical power in the universe. This power is transcendent but the religion is actually quite personal.

John: What do you mean by personal?

George: Well firstly one must understand that the faith they have in the power transcends this world and everything in it. This is even greater than the ethics one has developed in stage 2. To makes sense of this Kierkegaard uses the biblical example of Abraham; he was commanded by God to kill his son Isaac, an act that is completely against all his ethics, and against all social norms. Yet Abraham was prepared to do this, because of his faith, he understood that what God wants transcends everything we understand, and we must have this complete faith in God. But more importantly we need to understand here, God's command to Abraham was not a law that would apply to all; it addressed Abraham as an individual, with an individual command.

John: I see.

George: So this religious faith needs to be on a personal basis. Kierkegaard claimed that the Christian faith is not just regurgitating church dogma. This was for, what Kierkegaard referred to as, "The Crowd". The usual way of seeing the world and seeing religion, with laws and rules that were universal. Kierkegaard actually said "the crowd is untruth." So the third stage is a matter of individual subjective passion something that cannot be offered by the church nor by scientific empirical fact.

John: Right.

George: Kierkegaard asks us to take a leap of faith in God, he actually refers to this as the absurd, because it cannot be quantified by any empirical means or objective fact. But what Kierkegaard is asking for is to have faith in a personal God. This stage, this faith is the most important task to be achieved by a human being, because only on the basis of this faith does an individual have a chance to become a true self. And so here is where Kierkegaard created the famous existential idea that subjectivity is truth, and the "single individual is higher than the universal."

John: Yes I understand.

George: So then the third and final stage to becoming your true self is faith in the absurd, have faith in the higher metaphysical existence of God. This will become a personal relationship with God, your faith will lead you to see yourself as an individual and new form of truth will arrive. Truth is not just a matter of objective facts, but the true self understands that subjectivity is truth. This will lead one to look inward, to distance themselves from the crowd and become an individual, to become their true self.

John: This is a fascinating theory, and I can really understand where Kierkegaard is coming from. I see the three stages mirrored in everyday life all the time. When we are young we are immersed in the aesthetic stage, we want to play with friends, we want to go out, we want to party etc. As we get older we are fully into the ethical stage, many people will get jobs, they will get married they will start a family get a mortgage etc. Here they develop their principles, they follow the law and social norms and immerse themselves in a wider community.

George: Yes.

John: And then as we get really old and we start to really think about our mortality we will take death a lot more seriously and may look for comfort in religion or spirituality.

George: Exactly, it is a very common path for people.

John: Some issues I have, firstly it seems the 3 stages are not applicable for atheists as you need develop faith in a deity.

George: Well they are applicable but an atheist will not reach stage 3, if they do not take the leap of faith then they can never be their true self.

John: Yes see I take issue with this, there are many spiritual, fulfilled or even enlightened atheists, they may not have faith in a Deity but I would say they have found their true self.

George: Well why won't an atheist take the leap of faith?

John: Because they do not see any evidence enough to have faith.

George: Exactly, the atheist is solely concerned with objective empirical fact; Kierkegaard would say this belongs to the crowd. What Kierkegaard is asking is to transcend this, the true individual must adopt a faith that cannot be verified or invalidated by science. Objective knowledge plays no part. If it did it wouldn't be faith. The reason it is the final stage is because it goes against our impulse of objectivity, it is faith in the absurd. So if the atheist is following the objective truths of the crowd then he will never reach stage 3.

John: Ok, fine but here's another problem, are the three stages universal?

George: What do you mean?

John: Does everyone need to pass through the three stages in order to become their true self, is this universal for all people?

George: Yes I think Kierkegaard would say so.

John: Ok, so in a way this becomes objective, it is the objective, universal formula that everyone must follow to become their true self. But how, in a theory that values subjectivity, can we have an objective universal formula. If

Subjectivity is truth, Kierkegaard relies on three objective stages to reach this, for me this seems like a contradiction

George: Hmmm.

John: If subjectivity is truth there shouldn't be any specific stages to becoming your true self. Every individual is different, every person is on a different path, with a different mind, in a different world, and so each individual's journey to becoming their true self would be different. If we are to really value subjectivity as truth we cannot quantify the path to truth, it would be impossible as it would be different for each person. So either subjectivity is truth or the 3 stages are the universal formula, but not both.

George: Interesting point.

Kierkegaard – The Knight of Faith

George: We shall now continue with Kierkegaard and look closer into the religious existentialism with a focus on the knight of faith. Now we all understand what it means to have faith in God, and to devote one's life to a higher being. However in his book fear and trembling, working under the pseudonym Johannes Silentio, the knight of faith is explained as someone who possesses the highest form of faith that one can have. The knight of faith is the epitome of the religious life, no matter the situation, the circumstance, the outcome, no matter what, they have complete and utter faith in God. Even when faced with logical contradictions, when ones faith is challenged by all reason and rationality one will still fully devote themselves to this faith. Kierkegaard refers to this as the absurd, when all reason and logic cannot explain the knight of faith will still hold onto this faith no matter what.

John: I'm not sure I understand this fully.

George: Ok to make things clearer, Kierkegaard gives the example of a knight of infinite resignation vs the knight of faith. In life we are met with challenges, with pain, with suffering, we want things we can't have, we can have things we love taken from us etc. When faced with such a challenge the knight of infinite resignation will be resigned to the fact of reality. They will accept that what they long for they cannot have in this life, they will be resigned to this fact, they will be resigned to their reality. It may cause them pain and trauma but they will accept it. The knight of faith will go through what the knight of infinite resignation goes through however they go one step further. They are resigned to the reality of their situation however they still believe what they want will be granted to them through the will of God. Even though it is impossible, even though they are resigned to the truth of the matter, they still have faith that in this life they will get what they long for, their faith continues even in the face of impossibility. This Kierkegaard refers to this as double movement. The knight of faith knows that they cannot achieve something, they give up on what they hold dear, yet at the same time they embrace the absurd, they embrace the illogical, they rise up and they say no matter the impossibility, no matter the irrationality, no matter the paradox, with faith in God anything can happen and what I long for can still be mine.

John: I see.

George: To illustrate this further Kierkegaard gives the example of the pauper falling in love with the princess. There is no way that in this lifetime the pauper will ever marry into the royal family, and so marrying the princess is a complete impossibility. Now, as a knight of infinite resignation the pauper will give up on marrying the princess, he may still hold onto this love, it will cause him pain and depression, he may even believe that they can be together in another life, however the pauper is resigned to the fact that they can never be together in this lifetime. However as soon as the pauper takes the final step, the double movement, he rises up and says I know I cannot marry the princess, I know it is a complete impossibility, yet I still have faith that I will marry the princess in this life, "I believe nevertheless that I shall get her, in virtue, that is, of the absurd, in virtue of the fact that with God all things are possible." Then the pauper becomes a knight of faith. The pauper has embraced the absurd; Kierkegaard refers to this as taking a leap of faith. Among the impossibility and paradox the pauper still believes. This is a knight of faith, this is what it means to have complete faith in God.

John: Very interesting.

George: Kierkegaard believed that the one person who has been the true personification of a knight of faith was Abraham, and this was made evident in the biblical story of the Binding of Isaac. In this story Abraham was instructed by God to sacrifice Isaac, God commanded Abraham to murder his son.

John: Ok, but how does this make Abraham a knight of faith.

George: Because Abraham was prepared to do this. Abraham was prepared to put his full faith in God, and commit this sacrifice even in the faith of all the paradoxes and absurdities. Abraham knew that murder was wrong, yet he knew that murdering his son was also right because he had the faith. Abraham loved his son and wanted the best for him, yet he was going to murder him, it was absurd, illogical it was pure faith. Abraham was prepared to murder his son yet at the same time he believed that everything would be fine, that his son would carry on living and would be blessed. This is the double movement, being prepared to murder your son but still believing they will survive, this is embracing absurdity, this is being a knight of faith.

John: Fascinating.

George: So there we have the knight of faith, a complete faith in God, even against all contradictions and reason, one carries on having the faith and believing that with faith in God everything will be ok, everything will be as it should.

John: Quite inspiring actually, I do get glimpses from religious people practicing this knight of faith concept when going through difficult times. Even in the most troubling of times, they will say God works in mysterious ways, they keep their faith intact. If anything it helps them carry on.

George: Yes indeed.

John: From a philosophical perspective I actually find Kierkegaard's knight of faith difficult to argue against. I'm always ready to debate using logic, and reason, but this particular theory specifically goes against logic and reason. It is actually the foundation of being a knight of faith, double movement and absurdity is by very their very nature illogical and that is the point. No matter what logical arguments I can throw to discredit the knight of faith, it doesn't really damage the nature of the theory because it is an illogical theory, you are supposed to have faith in the unreasonable and contradictory. This seems difficult to argue against. Granted I would never be convinced to be a knight of faith as I value logic over faith, but I cannot use logic to argue against a theory that values faith over logic.

George: Interesting point.

John: The only thing I would say, not from a philosophical point of view but more a societal point of view, is that the knight of faith concept can actually be quite dangerous.

George: How so?

John: If someone is willing to give up all reason and rationality for their faith then what else are they prepared to do? Abraham was willing to kill his son, his faith allowed him to discard all morality and emotion and do what God commanded. Can this not be used to excuse any evil behaviour? What if someone truly believes that God wants them to commit acts of terrorism, murder, genocide etc. No matter how you argue on a moral level, on a logical level, on an emotional level, on a human level, it will not matter, as they can simultaneously think that their evil acts will be fine as they have faith. I think this can open the door to religious extremism of the worst kind, and can justify just about anything as long as you have faith.

George: Very well put, and this concludes our philosophy of religion discussion.

The Philosophy Vibe Anthology

Volume 1: Philosophy of Religion

Volume 2: Metaphysics

Volume 3: Ethics and Political Philosophy

Printed in Great Britain
by Amazon

37123403R00086